# Mindfulness

*and the*
## Big Questions

# Mindfulness
*and the*
## BIG QUESTIONS

Ben Irvine

*Leaping Hare Press*

First published in the UK in 2017 by
*Leaping Hare Press*
An imprint of The Quarto Group
The Old Brewery, 6 Blundell Street
London N7 9BH, United Kingdom
**T** (0)20 7700 6700 **F** (0)20 7700 8066
www.QuartoKnows.com

Text © 2017 Ben Irvine
Design and layout © 2017 Quarto Publishing plc

British Library Cataloguing-in-Publication Data
A catalogue record for this book is available from the
British Library

ISBN: 978-1-78240-430-9

This book was conceived, designed and produced by
*Leaping Hare Press*
58 West Street, Brighton BN1 2RA, United Kingdom

*Publisher* Susan Kelly
*Creative Director* Michael Whitehead
*Editorial Director* Tom Kitch
*Commissioning Editor* Monica Perdoni
*Designer* Wayne Blades

Printed in China

10 9 8 7 6 5 4 3 2 1

A note from the author:
In this book, when mentioning a person but no person in particular, I
have opted to use the masculine form (for no other reason than that I am
a man) but, of course, the points I am making address all people equally.

# Contents

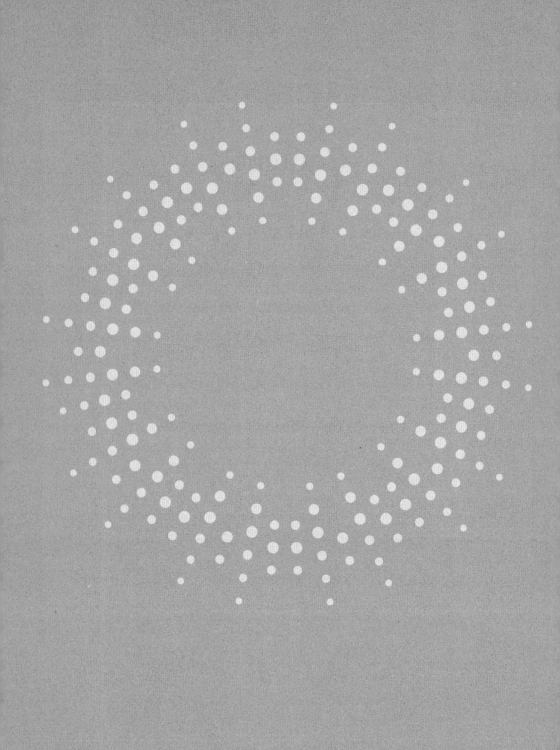

# One

## Hidden in Plain Sight

A man stands on a bridge, his hands clasped to his ears, his ghostly face a mask of dread. Behind him, ominously, a swirling red sky is blending into a dark blue sea; everything is dissolving into everything else. Edvard Munch's famous painting *The Scream* expresses a mood many of us know only too well: existential anxiety, a fear of our very existence. For many years, I suffered from existential anxiety. I became obsessed with the Big Questions, searching high and low for answers that might help me come to terms with my life. This book describes how I found what I was looking for, and how you can too, in a most surprising place. The answers, it turns out, are hiding in plain sight. And they come alive in mindfulness.

The feeling of existential anxiety is hard to put into words. When you're afraid of your existence, there's no particular thing you fear – you fear everything, yourself included. You feel as though you've been kidnapped and abandoned in a strange, terrifying place where nothing makes sense, where you don't belong, where you don't trust your judgement or your decisions. You're desperate to find a way to cope with the situation. What do you do?

When I first developed existential anxiety, in my late teens, I did what most people do when they're afraid: I tried to hide. Obviously, you can't literally hide from your existence, but you can distract yourself from it, by distracting yourself from your own mind and from reality. To this end, I drank lots of beer, danced in nightclubs and played video games all day.

When I look around these days, I still see lots of people trying to distract themselves from their existence. Not just through drinking or gaming but through television, smartphones, social media, gambling, celebrity gossip and drugs. Judging by the popularity of these various distractions, I suppose there is a pandemic of existential anxiety in the modern world.

The problem with distracting yourself from life is that you only worsen your existential anxiety. Hiding from a situation makes you exaggerate what you fear, to justify your hiding. And when you waste time on distractions, you neglect your life, and your life becomes chaotic, and your sense of dismayed confusion grows.

That's what happened to me. In my distractedness, I messed up my college exams, got beaten up while drunk, and started having panic attacks. I soon realised I needed a better way to deal with my existential anxiety. Instead of hiding from my existence, I decided to try to understand it –

life, the universe, the whole damn thing. I craved a sense of meaning, a way to turn my worries into a more uplifting world view. So I turned to the Big Questions.

## Wising Up

Why am I here? Do I really know anything? Am I free? Is there a higher power? What makes a life good? What does it all mean?

We all ask the Big Questions from time to time; they are a natural response to being alive. We want to know why we exist, what is happening around us, what power we have over our situation, who (if anyone) put us here and what their intentions were, why such a place as this exists, how best to deal with it and each other, and what steps we can take to find solace. And we want to know how all these answers fit together into an overall explanation of existence.

That's not too much to ask, is it? Well, it was definitely too much for me to figure out on my own. I sought help, from the experts – expert Big Questioners, otherwise known as 'philosophers'. The word philosophy combines the Greek roots 'philo' and 'sophos', meaning, respectively, 'love' and 'wisdom'. A philosopher, accordingly, is a 'lover of wisdom'.

Wisdom: it was precisely what I needed. I was an existential neophyte, frightened and unsure, shying away from life; in contrast, a wise person is well informed and well adjusted, someone who looks long and hard at life, who doesn't blink, and who makes the right moves. It seemed to me that if I could get to grips with the Big Questions, and find satisfying answers, I could wise up to my existence.

That's pretty much how philosophers throughout history have viewed their vocation. According to various famous thinkers, philosophy starts in a sense of 'uprootedness' (Martin Heidegger), 'astonishment' (Socrates) or 'fear and trembling' (Søren Kierkegaard) – in other words, philosophy starts in existential anxiety – but finally leads to wisdom.

So I resolved to learn from the experts; I read and read and read, and thought and thought and thought. My studies took me into many fields of enquiry where philosophers have made contributions, not just in philosophy itself but in religion, sociology and psychology. Indeed, I took my studies so seriously, I soon became an expert; I completed a PhD in philosophy.

There was just one problem: the truth is, most philosophers hate wisdom.

## The Big Distractions

How many philosophers does it take to change a lightbulb? According to the popular joke, the answer is three: one to change the lightbulb, the other two to argue about whether the lightbulb exists or not. Yes, we all occasionally laugh at philosophers, those over-thinking, beard-scratching, navel-gazing, self-obsessed, work-shy nit-pickers who live on another planet and disappear up their own backsides. I used to find these stereotypes annoying. But now I think the cynics are onto something.

I studied philosophy for over a decade. Gradually, a troubling realisation dawned on me. The realisation was subtle, and for that reason it will take time to explain throughout this book. For now, it can be summarised as follows: *most philosophers ask the Big Questions in utterly the wrong way.*

Typically, philosophers don't try to make sense of human existence. Rather, they deny human existence. They come up with Big Answers that shun the here and now – answers that shun the human mind, shun reality, or shun both. In other words, most philosophers use the Big Questions as a form of distraction; they come up with Big Answers that are just a highbrow way of not paying attention to existence, of hiding from existential anxiety. No wonder philosophers have a reputation for being otherworldly.

Of course, not everyone is cynical about philosophy. Many people believe – sometimes with good reason – that philosophers are the deepest and profoundest of thinkers. But I suspect that often people are simply bamboozled by philosophy. When philosophers talk about existence in highly counterintuitive terms, people assume – falsely – that these philosophers must be saying things about existence that are too profound to understand.

As far as the man in the street is concerned, a person who is being 'philosophical' says something like: 'I'm aware of the situation I'm in, I understand what I'm facing, I'm coming to terms with it, and I'm dealing with it.' In this sense, most philosophers are not very philosophical, and – which is pretty much the same thing – not very wise.

For a long time, I was one of the unwise philosophers. But gradually I started to do things differently, properly. In the end, I came up with a new way of asking the Big Questions. Quite simply, I assumed that the answers must be life-affirming, not life-denying. I soon unearthed some homely but inspiring findings – some Small Answers to the Big Questions.

In the chapters that follow, I will share these Small Answers with you, and I will share such wisdom as can be gained from them. But there's another side to the story – the most important part.

When I finally left academic philosophy, I felt that I had a better understanding of my existence than ever before, yet I still didn't feel comfortable being alive. My existential anxiety was continuing to gnaw at me. It was time to go back to basics.

## Rediscovering Mindfulness

You don't have to know what mindfulness is to be mindful. Before I ever knew there was a word for it, I experienced a few sporadic episodes of mindfulness in my life. I remember one above all.

I was sitting on some black rocks on the shore of Lindisfarne Island, looking across to the Northumberland coast. The North Sea was calm and flat, punctuated only by two seals ducking and gliding in the water. I watched those seals for ages. I felt completely at peace, with the world and with myself. My thoughts and feelings came and went, flickering and fading like the soft morning light skittering on the water's surface; I was aware of them, yet I was undistracted by them. My focus belonged only to those two seals, and the sea, and the smudge of land on the horizon beyond.

When mindfulness became popular in the early twenty-first century, I wondered, like most people, 'what's this about?'. I picked up a guidebook, and was surprised to discover that I was actually rediscovering something.

Mindfulness is the simple act of paying attention to your experience, while also cultivating a conscious aloofness towards your thoughts, sensations and feelings. When I was sitting on the shore of Lindisfarne, mindfulness came naturally to me, and I'm sure you can think of times in your life when you've experienced a natural form of mindfulness. But we can't spend all our time watching seals, knitting jumpers, hang-gliding or doing whatever it is that makes us naturally mindful. Instead, we can muster up a state of mindfulness anywhere and anytime by deliberately paying attention to an aspect of our current experience. This deliberate effort is known as 'meditation'.

As a beginner in meditation, you are usually encouraged to focus your attention on your breathing, while taking deep, long, calm breaths. You can focus on the air as it enters and exits your nostrils or mouth, or on your ribcage or diaphragm as it rises and falls, but all the while you try to keep your focus fixed. If your thoughts wander, or your attention strays, you simply bring your focus back to your breathing. You don't beat yourself up about your wandering mind – wandering is what minds do.

And you don't try to push away any of your thoughts, sensations or feelings. You just let them have their moment; simply notice them, like patterns of light on water, then gently bring your attention back to your breathing.

Experienced meditators focus on all manner of experiences, including their own bodies, other objects, colours, scenes or sounds. Sometimes people even meditate on the move – say, while walking or cycling. But, in all these variations, deep, calm breathing is a central part of meditation – a cushion, if you like, for your attention to rest on.

Of course, meditating isn't quite the same thing as serenely gazing at the sea. Deliberate focus requires discipline. Yet, even as you put the effort in, meditation ushers in that same calm, attentive state of mind that I experienced on Lindisfarne: a state, in other words, of mindfulness. Through meditating, we can bootstrap ourselves into mindfulness – and not

**"Through meditating, we can bootstrap ourselves into mindfulness"**

just while we're meditating. Mindfulness becomes a habit, bringing greater calmness and focus to every area of our lives.

As I rediscovered mindfulness, as I followed the meditation exercises recommended by the guidebooks, as I recalled those rare episodes in my life when I had been naturally mindful, I was struck by one thing above all, something potentially life-changing for me and others like me: *mindfulness is the very opposite of existential anxiety*. After all, breathing deeply and calmly is the opposite of being afraid, and calmly paying attention to your experience is the opposite of hiding from life.

I had finally found the cure to my fear of existence. I had found what I was looking for as a philosopher – including some old findings in an exciting new form.

## A Familiarity Meditation

Throughout this book I am going to invite you to try some bespoke 'philosophical' meditations. First of all, though, I'd like to familiarise you with the basics of meditation – hence the name of this particular exercise. I've also used the word 'familiarity' for two other reasons.

The first is that I expect you'll find mindfulness familiar, just as it was to me. No matter how much existential anxiety you've experienced in the past, I bet you can think of a time when you felt naturally mindful.

The second reason is that I want you to see this exercise as a way of deliberately familiarising yourself with being alive. If you're someone who suffers from existential anxiety, if you've been hiding from your existence, then mindfulness meditation will help you return to the here and now. By focusing mindfully on being here now, hopefully you'll see that your existence is not as scary as you thought.

The customary way to introduce newcomers to meditation – through a simple breathing exercise – is the perfect way for us to begin. Breathing has a calming effect, which will add further reassurance to your growing sense of familiarity with your existence. And, since breathing is the very basis of being alive, when you focus on your breathing you'll be squarely facing up to your existence rather than hiding from it.

It's a good idea to use a timer while meditating. If you have a timer, set it to beep in about ten minutes' time. Then sit on a hard chair, with your back straight, and place your palms gently on your thighs. You can keep your eyes open or shut – whichever you prefer. Now simply breathe, slowly and deeply, while focusing intently on each breath as it enters and exits your mouth or nostrils. Really observe what each breath feels like, as though the sensation of breathing were the only thing in the universe that mattered. If a thought pops into your head, just acknowledge it – 'oh, there goes a thought' – and bring your attention back to your breathing. Whenever your attention wanders (and it will) just acknowledge where it has wandered to – 'ah, there are my toes' – then bring your focus back to your breathing.

Ten minutes of pure existence. It's not so bad, is it?

## Getting Clear

They can race. They can idle. They can free you. They can be pressing. They can be elsewhere. They can be pertinent. They can be repetitive. They can be original. They can be abstract. They can be penetrating. They can be useful or satisfying or wander pleasantly, or they can be frightening. You can share them. You can conceal them. You can have a train of them. You can lose your train of them. They define you as a human being, but sometimes they make no sense at all. They are strange, these things we call thoughts. They can even be bewildering. We can get lost in them, entangled in them, overcome by them.

Mindfulness meditation has helped millions of people recover from psychological problems such as depression, anxiety, obsessive compulsive disorder (OCD), phobias and post-traumatic stress disorder. Mental distress typically consists in persistent negative patterns of thinking. For instance, a depressed person might spend much of his time ruminating: 'I'm a failure; look at all the times I've failed in the past; I'll probably fail again in the future.' Or a person with OCD might be tormented by intrusive thoughts such as: 'I must wash my hands again; they're covered in germs; I've been touching dirty surfaces.'

When suffering from mental distress, we get tangled up in negative thoughts, as though we are lost in dense undergrowth and struggling to find a way out. The more we worry about our predicament, the more frantically and blindly we try to escape, and the deeper we go into confusion and dismay. There is a vicious cycle connecting our negative thoughts and our negative emotions. Whenever we think negative thoughts, we feel fear, sadness, frustration or anger, and, in turn, these emotions make us think negatively.

Mindfulness helps us escape from mental distress by teaching us how to distance ourselves from our thoughts. In deliberately focusing on our breathing, and in letting our thoughts come and go as they please, we come to realise that the part of our mind that pays attention is separate from whatever it pays attention to, just as a singer is separate from his song. Our attention creates a 'clearing' within our own minds. In this clearing, our thoughts surround us, but they don't engulf us. We realise that our thoughts don't have to affect us if we don't want them to. We can break out of the cycle of negativity.

Of course, meditation isn't the last word in psychotherapy. There are other ways of dealing with negative thoughts than distancing ourselves from them. In cognitive behavioural therapy (CBT), people with psychological problems are encouraged to challenge their negative thoughts using logic and evidence. A depressed person might learn to think: 'I'm not a failure; I've enjoyed plenty of successes in my life; and, anyway, my future doesn't have to resemble my past.' Or a person with OCD struggling with a fear of germs might learn to think: 'My hands are already clean; and, anyway, a few little germs won't really hurt me.' If mindfulness is like creating a clearing in the undergrowth, then CBT is like beating a path through the undergrowth.

Contrary to first appearances, mindfulness and CBT are not opposed to each other – in fact, they are complementary. Distancing ourselves from our negative thoughts can help us challenge them. When we recognise that our thoughts are 'only' thoughts, it's easier to appreciate that they might be false or misleading. Indeed, many psychotherapists advocate a hybrid approach called mindfulness-based cognitive therapy (MBCT). The mindfulness aspect of MBCT helps patients to avoid getting tangled up when they are in the process of challenging their thoughts, while the CBT aspect encourages patients not to numbly acquiesce in negative thoughts.

My Small Answers to the Big Questions are like a course of CBT for people who suffer from existential anxiety. When we follow the example of most philosophers – when we distract ourselves from existence by hiding in life-denying answers to the Big Questions – we deliberately lose ourselves in tangled thickets of thought. Through my life-affirming Small Answers, I learned to beat a path through the confusion of life-denying philosophy. Yet, until I rediscovered mindfulness, I was still somewhat tangled up in the Big Questions. I was turning the Small Answers over and over in my mind, like a record player on loop. Meditation helped me create an inner space whereby I could distance myself from my chronic philosophising. And in that space something amazing happened: I really experienced the Small Answers – not just abstractly, but vividly and directly. The Small Answers came alive through my mindful experience.

And so did I: my existential anxiety gave way to wisdom and happiness. Mindfulness was the ingredient I had been missing. But this doesn't mean that we should give up on philosophy altogether. I overcame my existential anxiety through the combination of mindfulness with my new life-affirming philosophy. The Small Answers are like the 3D image hidden in a Magic Eye picture. To learn to see the image – and, likewise, to learn to see the Small Answers vividly and directly – you need some verbal prompting. You need to learn *how* to see. Life-affirming philosophy can help us get the most out of mindfulness, and vice versa.

And there is another reason for not giving up on philosophy. The truth is, if we don't think about mindfulness in the right way, meditation itself can become a form of distraction.

## Meaningful Meditation

Just as there are stereotypes about philosophers, there are stereotypes about people who meditate regularly. Interestingly, the two sets of stereotypes are similar. Supposedly, meditators are naive, idealistic, empty-headed, self-obsessed, navel-gazing hippies who live on another planet with their heads in the clouds and who shun society and hate modern life.

Once again, I must confess that these stereotypes are onto something. Since I've become interested in mindfulness, I've met lots of people who use meditation as a way of distracting themselves from, rather than facing up to, existence. Instead of training themselves to embrace being here now, some meditators consider the practice to be a way of escaping to an imaginary better place. This life-denying form of meditation is nicely illustrated in a scene from the film *Fight Club*. The main character attends a group meditation class during which the session leader tells her mesmerised students, 'you're going deep into your cave'.

No wonder there's so much overlap between the stereotypes of meditators and the stereotypes of philosophers. Indeed, the people who use meditation to distract themselves from existence also tend to be drawn to life-denying philosophy. They advocate answers to the Big Questions that attempt to transport us to another realm, a realm where human existence is something other than what it is.

Because mindfulness originates in Buddhist philosophy, especially in the sayings and writings of various sages from India and China, meditators tend to approach the Big Questions via this 'Eastern' tradition. However, as we will see, there is much that is similar between Western and Eastern philosophy. Both traditions are replete with life-denying theories of existence. Both traditions, I think, would benefit from some Small Answers to the Big Questions.

In the chapters that follow, we'll learn the dos and don'ts of Eastern and Western philosophy, and of meditation. We'll learn how to use philosophy and meditation not as a way of distracting ourselves from life but as a way of prompting us to see human existence for what it is. We'll cultivate mindfulness through cultivating a philosophy of mindfulness, and through meditating mindfully not life-denyingly. We'll tackle the Big Questions not by getting lost in confusion but by looking for Small Answers that are hidden in plain sight. And, in so doing, we'll transform our existential anxiety into its opposite. We'll learn how to stand on that same bridge depicted in Munch's painting – with that same swirling red sky blending into that same dark blue sea, with everything dissolving into everything else. But we won't feel the need to scream. We'll be calm, focused, mindful – living meaningfully in the here and now.

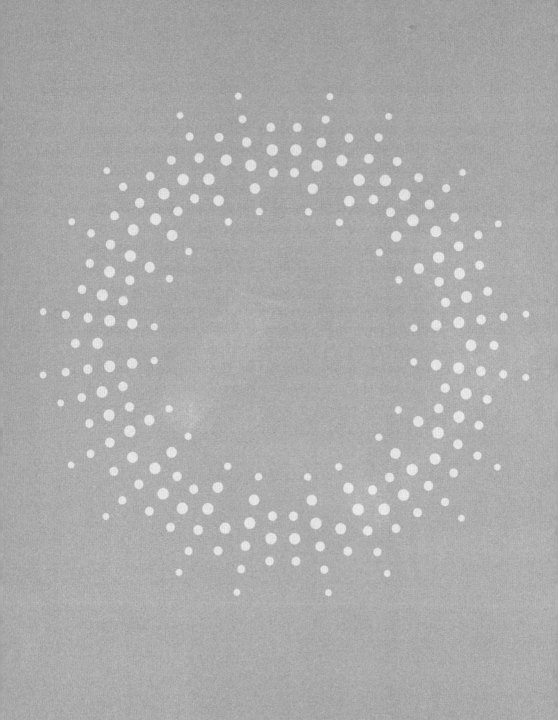

# Two

# Why Am I Here?

'I am here now' is true of each and every one of us, for every moment of our waking lives. Yet it's a truth many of us find hard to understand, and even harder to accept. In a futile attempt to get our heads around being here now, we explore philosophies, religions and ideologies that promise to carry us away from our existence, to show us who we 'really' are, deep down. We are like drunks trying to drink ourselves sober. To appreciate what being here now really means, we don't need to hide from our existence. Quite the opposite: we simply need to see more clearly who and where we are.

I was about eight years old when it first hit me. My mum had asked me to post a letter in the postbox at the top of our road. I was standing beside the postbox, my arm outstretched, when suddenly I had a disconcerting thought: why am *I* in my body? The postbox didn't have a person inside it (as far as I knew). Nor did the envelope in my hand (well, not exactly). Yet there I was – sending instructions to my arm, peering out of my skull, wondering how the heck I got in there. I dropped the letter through the slot and ran home as fast as I could.

Unfortunately, it wasn't quite so easy to leave behind my confusion about being me. Periodically throughout my childhood I felt that I was haunting my body like a ghost. Sometimes I wondered why I wasn't in someone else's body, or why I wasn't in some other object, such as a tree. Other times I wondered why my body didn't contain someone other than me, or why it contained anyone at all.

I was soon relieved to discover that I wasn't the only self-haunting person in the world. When I started reading philosophy books in my late teens, I learned that people have been confused about an entity called the 'self' for as long as there have been people.

The self is what we refer to when we say 'myself' or when we say 'I'. Each of us has a self. Philosophers talk about *the* self in the same way that a physician talks about the body: we've all got one (of each). Yet having a self is in many ways completely different from having a body. There are some features of the self that appear very ghostly indeed.

Consider, for instance, the fact that your self gives you complete privacy. No one else but you will ever gain access to your self. You and only you will ever know what happens inside your self. Relatedly, your self also gives you a viewpoint that no one else will ever share. Only you can look out of the little porthole of your self. Only you can ever see the world as you see it – and, indeed, you cannot see the world other than as you see it. For these reasons, your self is what makes you an individual – an individual person with a private inner view of the world. In turn, your self is the source of your decisions in life, these decisions being based on your private viewpoint. You bear individual responsibility for those decisions simply because – not being you – no one else could have made them.

Your self is so essential to who you are, you don't just *have* a self – you *are* your self. This grammatical ambiguity reflects our human capacity for 'self-awareness'. In self-awareness, you are aware of the self that you have, and simultaneously this awareness is something that your self does. You are a self that can be aware of itself.

If that isn't confusing enough, the self also has a confusing relationship to the rest of reality. Your self occupies your body, or, more specifically, your brain. Yet – apart from the human brain – every object in the universe has characteristics that are the very opposite of the self's. Every object can be viewed by anyone. There are no fundamental restrictions on who gets to view Jupiter, the Eiffel Tower, this book or anything else. The universe is like a vast museum in which all the objects are on public display. And, of course, in this museum, as in any other, the exhibited objects don't make decisions by themselves. Some of them move around, yes, but none of them – including, presumably, animals – are under the command of a self-aware private spectator.

Except for the human brain. Somehow your brain has it both ways. It is an object on display like any other object – anyone can open up your skull and look at your brain, and, in doing so, they won't be able to access its private inner viewpoint or decision-making powers – yet there *you* are, inside your brain, with precisely that kind of access. Another way of making the same point is: the human brain has no special properties that distinguish it from the rest of the universe – brain cells are made out of the same chemical elements as any other object, and operate by the same laws of physics – yet the human brain harbours a self that obviously is one of a kind.

As a child I had become dimly aware of what Western philosophers call the 'explanatory gap' between the human brain and the self. The self and the human brain are so different there can be no explanation of why an individual person occupies a particular brain as opposed to occupying any other object, or any other brain, or no object at all.

I thought I was a ghost – and I was spooked. If only I knew then what I know now: spooking yourself is a very silly thing to do.

## Estranged from Life

How would you feel if you arrived home to find a stranger sitting on your doorstep? And what would you think if that stranger immediately insisted you should embrace him as a friend? Chances are, your gut feeling would be: don't trust him; be afraid.

Sadly – or, perhaps, sensibly – when we're confronted by a stranger, we often experience a pang of scepticism and fear. We feel that if the stranger wants us to trust him then the burden of proof is on his shoulders. Some people – misanthropists – demand an impossibly high level of proof before trusting anyone. A misanthropist treats every word that comes out of a stranger's mouth as suspicious.

And, of course, some strangers are stranger than others. If the man on your doorstep was behaving in an especially erratic or confusing manner, you'd be even less likely to trust him, and more likely to fear him.

Confusion about being here now is a powerful source of existential anxiety. When we reflect on how different the self and reality are, we get the impression that we don't really belong here now; we feel estranged from the world. We feel that our existence is – well, strange. This sense of strangeness leads us to distrust and fear our existence. We fearfully refuse to take our lives at face value. We instinctively assume that being here now is not the truth.

> **"Confusion about being here now is a powerful source of existential anxiety"**

Of course, for some people this distrust of life is temporary or intermittent. But for others, existential anxiety becomes entrenched. Some people suffer from such severe existential anxiety they treat their lives as suspicious almost constantly. This is true of many philosophers – and it was once true of me.

Philosophers who are chronically anxious can be useful, however. For one thing, they inadvertently showcase existential anxiety in its most florid and vivid form, which can teach the rest of us how not to react to being here now. And because some philosophers are so good at clarifying their ideas, we can study philosophy to get a clear understanding of the negative thought patterns through which people try to escape from existence.

The fundamental starting point of most philosophers – Eastern and Western – is to reject the statement 'I am here now'. Logically there are various ways for the statement to be false. Philosophers tend to pick one of these options and argue trenchantly for it. Throughout this book, we'll look in more detail at these options. For now, a quick overview will suffice.

Philosophers who champion 'none-sided' theories of existence claim that 'I am here now' is false because *neither* the self nor reality exists.

Sometimes these philosophers conjure up an alternative entity; other times they just conclude that nothing exists.

Philosophers who champion 'one-sided' theories of existence claim that *either* the self or the world exists, but not both. Some of these philosophers claim that only the world exists, not the self, while others claim that only the self exists, not the world.

Philosophers who champion 'two-placed' theories of existence claim that the self and the world both exist, but in completely separate places. The self, accordingly, is not here now but ... somewhere else.

Philosophers who champion 'three-sided' theories of existence claim that the self and reality both exist but only as manifestations of a third thing. Because the third thing is an entity beyond the self and beyond the world, these philosophers say that 'I am here now' is, strictly speaking, false. The third thing is sometimes identified with God, or – especially in Eastern philosophy – with a mystical realm of some kind.

Did you spot what was missing? That's right: a 'two-sided' theory of existence. Unlike you, most philosophers ignore this option. A two-sided theory *accepts* rather than rejects the truth of 'I am here now'. If 'I am here now' is true, then the self exists and the world exists but not in separate places; the self and the world are two 'sides' or aspects of one and the same existence.

The notion that human existence has two sides – the self and the world – is simply too strange for most philosophers to contemplate. Like misanthropists, these philosophers turn their backs on what they fear, ruminating anxiously all the while.

To come to terms with being here now, to overcome existential anxiety, we need to learn to trust our experience. Instead of refusing to take our existence at face value – instead of constantly second-guessing what our existence is 'really' telling us – we need to pay attention, fearlessly and openly, to being here now. If our existence seems to have two sides, so be it; let's find out more about what that means. In the end, the only way to make a stranger seem less strange is to get to know him – and the only way to make our existence seem less strange is to deliberately acquaint ourselves with it. In doing so, we might even come to embrace life.

## Two Sides of Life

Without further ado, here's the Small Answer to why you're here: you are here because your brain has a selfside and a worldside.

In the introductory chapter, I claimed that the Small Answers to the Big Questions are like a course of CBT for sufferers of existential anxiety, and I promised that I would show how the Small Answers come alive in mindfulness. So first of all let me explain what I mean by the 'two sides' of your existence, before I invite you to meditate on what we've learned.

To help with this process, I'd like to invite you to create a simple prop. (Or, if you prefer, you can create the prop 'in your mind's eye'.) I'd like you to cut out a circle of plain paper. On one side of the circle, write the word 'self'. On the other side, write the word 'world'. That's all.

What you've created is a model human brain. The model shows how a single entity can have two sides that cancel each other out. Turn the circle of paper over in your hands. When the selfside is facing you – when it is 'prominent' – the worldside is 'recessive'. And, contrariwise, when the worldside is prominent, the selfside is recessive. In a sense, a recessive side of the circle stops existing in its own right; it becomes a mere part of the prominent side. Yet, in another sense, a recessive side of the circle continues to exist in its own right, because the circle continues to have two sides, regardless of which of them is prominent.

Here's another way to put the same point: the two sides of the circle oppose each other only because they are also a part of each other. The selfside is *not* the worldside, and the worldside is *not* the selfside; yet, at the same time, the selfside *is* the worldside, and vice versa, because each is part of the other. Together the selfside and the worldside form a unitary whole even though they are opposites. They are 'two and the same', you could say.

Now let's apply this same pattern to the human brain, taking *your* brain as our example. On the one hand, your brain is an object like any other object, on public display, part of the world's vast museum of objects. On the other hand, your brain harbours your self, with the private viewpoint and decision-making powers that you and only you can access. In other words, your brain has two sides: a selfside and a worldside.

These two sides of your brain oppose each other; your self is the very opposite of the world, and the world is the very opposite of your self. When you are self-aware, your self becomes prominent and the world recedes. The world becomes a mere part of your self-awareness; the world becomes your viewpoint. Alternatively, when you are not self-aware – when you are 'absent-minded', as it were – the world becomes prominent and your self recedes. Your self becomes a mere part of the world. Yet, because your self and the world are a part of each other, each continues to exist even when the other is prominent; they form a unitary whole. The two sides of your brain are two and the same.

Obviously, your brain doesn't have 'sides' in the same way that a paper circle has sides; you can't flip your brain over in your hands to see its two sides. The paper circle is only an analogy. Your self and the world are two sides of existence, two different – albeit unified – ways of being.

Nor does the circle analogy mean that your self and the world occupy different places. Contrary to 'two-placed' theories of existence, your self and the world are not in separate realms. You are here now. Your self is in the world, like any other object, because your self is a side of your brain.

But why? Why does the human brain have two sides? Have we *really* bridged the 'explanatory gap' between the self and the world? Well, no we haven't; we've done something better. We've explained why the explanatory gap exists. If the self and the world are like two sides of a paper circle, then it is obvious why we can't explain why the self and the world coexist. After all, you can't explain why the two sides of a paper circle coexist either!

Try it: you'll find that your mind flounders. When you think about the fact that the two sides of the circle oppose each other, you'll find that there's no way to 'get' from one to the other. They're utterly different: there's nothing about one of the sides that can explain the other side. Alternatively, when you think about the fact that the two sides of the circle are unified, your mind still struggles to explain why. Each side is the other side: asking why this is the case is like asking why the sun is the sun.

> **"Your self and the world are not in separate realms. You are here now"**

By explaining that the brain has a selfside and a worldside, we've explained why there is an explanatory gap between the self and the world. The self and the world are opposites – and therefore mutually incomprehensible. And the unity of the self and the world can no more be explained than the sun's unity with itself.

As well as explaining the explanatory gap, a two-sided brain can help us clear up another mystery: the mystery of how you can *have* a self and *be* a self. Your brain 'has' a self because your brain has a selfside. But, simultaneously, your brain *is* its selfside, just as one side of a paper circle *is* its other side. In other words, when your brain is aware of itself, it is aware that it *is* the self that it *has*. And – of course – that self is you! You are the self that your brain has and is. So everything we have said about the brain is true of your self, too. You *are* the self that you *have*.

Confused? Don't worry. It can take a while to get used to the theory that existence is two-sided. We've got a while to go in this book.

For now, let's have a breather – and a eureka moment.

## The River and the Oasis

In mindfulness, we decline to get tangled up in our thoughts. By focusing on a particular aspect of our experience – say, our breathing – while allowing our thoughts to come and go as they please, we become highly aware of the contents of our minds and highly aware of our existence in the world. In doing so, we enter into a lovely state that could be described as 'self-aware awareness'. When we're mindful, we're aware of the world around us while also being aware of ourselves being aware of the world.

When I first starting practising mindfulness, I was delighted to discover that self-aware awareness perfectly encapsulated my two-sided theory of human existence.

For one thing, in mindfulness the abstract idea of a prominent self really comes alive; you vividly experience your self as prominent. Indeed, your task in mindfulness is to *keep* your self prominent, keep being self-aware.

But, of course, there is more to mindfulness than being self-aware: mindfulness is self-aware *awareness* – that is, awareness of reality. After all, the world doesn't go anywhere when it recedes behind your self-awareness. The world stays right there, overlaid by your self. In mindfulness, your task is to see *through* your self-awareness to reality, as though seeing through glass. You keep your self prominent, but you also anchor your attention to the recessive world beyond your self, as though you are pressing your face to the glass.

In other words, reality, too, comes alive in mindfulness. Through our self-aware awareness, we vividly, not just abstractly, understand that the world exists even as it is overlaid by our self-awareness. Indeed, in mindfulness our experience of reality is *enhanced* by our self-awareness, as though the self were a spotlight illuminating our surroundings.

In this way, mindfulness encapsulates the idea that the self and the world are two and the same. When we are mindful, we experience the self and the world *together* even though the two are opposites. We appreciate vividly the truth of 'I am here now'.

Ironically, when I first started practising mindfulness, one of the clearest indications that my two-sided theory of existence was correct was that I felt I had no further need for the theory. I felt as though I had been carried by a river to an oasis. In mindfulness, I stopped deliberately thinking about the two sides of existence. I stopped turning them over in my mind's eye; I stopped obsessively thinking about the self and the world, and about their connectedness. Instead, I simply focused on being here now. If any thoughts about my existence occurred to me, I allowed them to fade away; they were but a pale imitation of the real thing, a pale imitation of actually being here now.

And the more I meditated, the calmer I felt. To me, this was the final and conclusive demonstration of my two-sided theory. I had originally aimed to overcome my existential anxiety by using philosophy to help me face up to being here now. In mindfulness, not only had I encountered clear and concrete evidence that my two-sided theory was correct, but my existential anxiety was indeed evaporating.

I am here now: I had seen enough strangeness to accept the obvious.

## The 'I Am Here Now' Meditation

This chapter has introduced a torrent of new ideas; we have jumped together into a river of philosophy. Thankfully, mindfulness brings this particular river to a calm conclusion, an oasis of self-aware awareness. I'd like to invite you now to meditate on what we've learned so far about being here now.

Just as before, prepare to sit up straight, and prepare to focus diligently and calmly on your breathing for ten minutes.

But this time, as you begin to focus on your breathing, I'd also like you to notice how your existence has two sides – a selfside and a worldside. Notice how these sides are two and the same. Notice your self-aware awareness. Notice the prominence of your self as you keep your attention trained on your breathing. Notice that you are here now.

Once you've noticed these things, let your mind gently drift into mindfulness. Let go of your thoughts. Let go of philosophy. If you find that your mind is wandering, if you find yourself thinking about the complexities of philosophy, or thinking about anything else, just bring your attention gently back to your breathing, and remind yourself: I am here now.

# Three

## Do I Really Know Anything?

Unless you're Mr Bean, everything that can go wrong won't necessarily go wrong: Murphy's Law is an exaggeration, thank goodness. But don't get cocky. As any good Boy Scout will tell you, what can go wrong might go wrong. In every situation we're in, and whatever course of action we take, uncertainty is ever-present. There are no guarantees that our plans will go to plan; the future might surprise us; our beliefs might be false. Whether we like it or not, uncertainty is in our nature, so if we want to come to terms with our lives, we'll have to learn more about the nature of uncertainty. Yet, in doing so, we can find genuine cause for confidence. We can transform insecurity into curiosity, anxiety into rationality, uncertainty into mindfulness.

Everyone remembers where they were on 11 September 2001, that dreadful day when terrorists attacked the US and killed thousands. I was in London, living at my parents' house. I had recently completed my undergraduate degree, and was enjoying settling back home. My mum and I were about to take our dog Daisy for an inoculation when the radio announcer said that a plane had crashed into the North Tower of the World Trade Center. By the time we had driven to the surgery, the TV in the reception was showing that the South Tower had been hit too; something awful was unfolding. We went into the consulting room, whereupon the vet plunged a syringe into Daisy's backside; she yelped. I've never forgotten that moment, with its absurd contrast to what was happening in New York. I realised then that everyday life – with its little errands, transactions and scenes – is fragile. Suddenly, every plane overhead sounded like a missile. Suddenly, there were known unknowns and unknown unknowns (as Donald Rumsfeld famously put it) everywhere. My existential anxiety went into overdrive; I went back to university to continue studying philosophy.

Uncertainty is like paraffin thrown upon the flames of fear. Unpleasant experiences are made more unpleasant by uncertainty; imagine, for instance, undergoing a painful dental procedure, during which the dentist suddenly says 'Oh, bloody hell, hang on …' then leaves the room for fifteen minutes without explanation (yes, this once happened to me). And when an unpleasant experience is a possibility, people often feel more afraid when they are not sure if the experience will come to pass or not than they do when they are sure that it will.

This last fact is not so surprising, when you think about it. In general, when you are told that something bad will happen – say, a severe storm – you reflect on your existing ability to cope, and you assess what else you could or should do to prepare. But when you are told only that something bad might happen, your uncertainty distracts you from thinking about preparations. You feel as much uncertainty about your ability to cope as you do about the event itself.

And, of course, you'd feel even worse if you were told that something bad might happen but nobody knows exactly what or when. That's why terrorism is so terrifying. With so much uncertainty in the air – much of it literally – after 11 September, US doctors reported a rise in demand for prescriptions for anxiety. Half of the respondents to a public survey reported that their 'sense of safety and security had been shaken'.

One of the most insidious effects of terrorism is that it turns previously anodyne situations into causes for alarm. In the wake of the many follow-up attacks that took place around the world after 11 September, people began to fear all manner of everyday objects. Cars, trucks, trains and planes might blow up or run amok. Envelopes might contain anthrax. Briefcases might conceal nuclear weapons. Bottles of liquid – potentially flammable – were banned from planes. Passengers' footwear had to be checked by airport security staff, following an incident in which a man tried to detonate explosives hidden in his shoes. One passenger was even caught with a bomb in his underpants ('Great Balls of Fire', declared the stoically humorous headline in the *New York Post*). Numerous flights made emergency landings when unattended mobile phones were found on board.

Of course, terrorism isn't the only generator of uncertainty in our lives. There are as many sources of uncertainty as there are things that can go wrong. And that's not even the half of our ignorance. At this moment, none of us has any idea, say, how many planets there are in the universe, or what our own planet will look like in a million years' time. But naturally most of us are more concerned about uncertainty in our proximate surroundings, where events and objects affect us directly.

To a large degree, our efforts in life aim to give us a sense of confidence. By 'confidence', I am referring to the nice feeling we have when we can manage our lives effectively because our circumstances are sufficiently predictable and dependable. We are like the character Truman Burbank in the film *The Truman Show*, who aspires to a life of routine and comfort in his pleasant home town of Seahaven. He kisses his wife goodbye as he leaves for work in the morning, smiles at his friendly neighbours, drives through clean and leafy streets to his cosy office job, and, in his spare time, hangs out with his trusty old pal Marlon.

Even thrill-seekers seek a sense of confidence to some extent. Extreme sportspeople check their equipment. Explorers take provisions. Sadomasochists trust each other not to go too far.

But no matter how hard we fight against it, uncertainty has a habit of casting a shadow over our lives. Our spouse or partner has an affair. The neighbours play loud music till the early hours. The alarm doesn't go off. The car won't start or the train is late. The boss says 'I'm gonna have to let you go'. Our friends don't return our calls. The rope gives way.

What can go wrong might go wrong – and often it does. Moreover, modern life has a habit of reminding us of this. The internet, by connecting us instantly to disasters everywhere, enables the media – and politicians – to serve up a daily diet of dire warnings. Terrorism is just the tip of the iceberg. There are so many people out there and so many things that can and do go wrong, our interconnected modern world makes Murphy's Law seem true.

We're also exposed to a barrage of antagonistic marketing these days, which further erodes our confidence. We're told that unless we buy some product or other, we'll look silly or, worse, we'll be in danger. Alas, we can't buy every product, so we're left feeling insecure. Or maybe we do try to buy every product, in which case we accrue debts, leaving us mired in financial uncertainty. Meanwhile, the wider economy, too, is dragged down by uncertainty, prompting well-meaning bureaucrats to use modern technology to meddle ever more intrusively, and unsettlingly, in our lives.

Above all, perhaps, many of us feel uncertain because we lack satisfying social relationships. Good relationships – with our family, friends, partners and neighbours – give us confidence, because our brains are designed for social living; together we can better predict and control our surroundings, because together we possess more eyes and ears and brain cells and limbs. But today family breakdown is more common than ever, with all the uncertainty this entails for children and parents. And community life in many areas is moribund. We spend time staring at screens instead of meeting face-to-face. The connectedness of the modern world is disconnecting us from each other. When we interact online, we are alone en masse.

Truman Burbank gradually lost confidence in his surroundings – for good reason. It turned out his whole life was fake. Everyone he ever encountered – his wife, his neighbours, his boss, everyone – was acting. They were characters in a TV show of which, unknowingly, he was the star. His beloved island town was merely a set. The film ends with him sailing away from the shore in a little boat, and arriving at the edge of a huge dome, the TV studio in which he has spent his life to date. For the star of *The Truman Show*, everything became uncertain.

The film remains popular because it touches a nerve. For many people, nothing much seems predictable or dependable; a sense of trust is hard to come by; even reality seems phoney. These people are on the edge. They think the world revolves around them. As we shall see, they're half right.

## The Menace of Self-absorption

In 1967, the psychologists Martin Seligman and Steven F. Maier made a fascinating discovery. They were conducting experiments on dogs, seeing how the poor mutts dealt with electric shocks. Some of the dogs learned to stop each shock by pressing a lever. Other dogs, however, had no such control, because they weren't given a lever; for them, the shocks stopped only when the *other* dogs pressed the lever. The discovery came when the experimenters placed all the dogs in a new setting, in which they could avoid further shocks simply by jumping over a small fence into a paddock where the floor wasn't electrified. The dogs that in the previous test had learned to press the lever soon learned to jump the fence. But – pitifully – the dogs that in the previous test had been unable to control the shocks simply lay down morosely, accepting their fate: more shocks.

The experimenters dubbed this phenomenon 'learned helplessness', the idea being that the dogs without a lever had learned to give up hope. It didn't take long for commentators to catch on to the eerie similarity between learned helplessness and various psychological problems that affect people. Of course, human beings are more complex than dogs. But any person can be overwhelmed by a sense of lacking control over his surroundings. When fear and uncertainty accumulate in such a person's life, a threshold of tolerance might soon be exceeded, whereupon he shrinks from his surroundings and says 'I can't control anything; I give up'. We might say that such a person has become depressed.

There are echoes of learned helplessness in other forms of dysfunctional human behaviour. A person with obsessive compulsive disorder retreats from life by locking himself into repetitive habits and tics; he creates for himself an illusion of control, because he believes that real control is unavailable to him. Similarly, albeit in a milder form, a person who procrastinates indulges in trivial distractions to avoid action. And a person who is addicted to drinking, drugs, video games or gambling gives up on life by retreating into an artificial world of someone else's design.

We can also develop learned helplessness through dysfunctional relationships, or simply through loneliness. The better the quality of our relationships, the more confident and independent we become. People who suffer abuse stay in an abusive relationship partly because their confidence has been eroded by their abuser.

Mentally distressed people often feel that the world has somehow become less real since they became unwell. Psychologists call this strange phenomenon 'derealisation'. One possible explanation for derealisation is that the more that people feel uncertain and out of control, the less they feel they understand what's happening around them. Reality starts to lose reality amid fearful uncertainty.

When learned helplessness and derealisation are combined, the result could be described as self-absorption. Self-absorbed people have a tenuous grip on the outside world; they spend much of their time wrapped up in their own thoughts and doubts. Such people can be found in all walks of life. But there is one group wherein an extreme and persistent form of self-absorption can be found. I am talking, of course, about philosophers.

## Existential Self-absorption

As we all know, philosophers tend to retreat from life. Many of them lack normal social contact. Many live as though in a dream, adrift of reality. This extreme derealisation takes two forms in philosophy.

The first is called 'scepticism'. The sceptic philosopher argues that we don't know anything of reality. He reasons as follows: if we did know anything of reality, we'd be in no doubt about it, because reality cannot be inherently uncertain, but, in fact, all our beliefs can be doubted, so we don't know anything of reality.

This conclusion strikes most people as excessive. Surely, wherever you are right now, the scene that you are surrounded by isn't entirely doubtful? Surely you cannot be mistaken that you're reading this book right now? The sceptic responds by coming up with hypothetical scenarios in which all our beliefs would indeed be false. One of the most memorable such scenarios was offered up by René Descartes. He asked us to consider the hypothesis that everything we experience is a trick being played on us by a powerful evil demon. We believe that we exist in the world, that we possess a body, that we perform activities such as reading books, whereas in actual fact the whole world, including our bodies, might be a sophisticated illusion conjured up by the demon. We can't prove that we're not being tricked in this way, say the sceptics; therefore we can't be certain that we know anything; therefore we don't know anything of reality.

Descartes also noted, however, that we do have at least one belief that definitely isn't the result of a trick: the belief that our self exists. After all, if you doubt that your self exists, then you immediately become sure that you do exist. Why so? Because if you're thinking you don't exist, then you must exist because it is *you* who is doing the thinking. 'I think therefore I am', is how Descartes famously put it.

Still, that's not much of a consolation. According to scepticism, the whole world drains away into uncertainty. All that remains is you – with all your beliefs, sensations and experiences amounting to nothing more than guesswork.

The second form of derealisation found within philosophy is even more extreme. Philosophers who call themselves 'idealists' deny that there is an external world to be certain about. Reality, so it goes, simply doesn't exist; there is no publicly accessible museum of objects. The beliefs, sensations and experiences that pass through the self – whoever's self that may be – are as real as it gets.

Although more extreme than scepticism, idealism is, in a way, more honest. The sceptic claims that knowledge of the world is possible, yet simultaneously denies that we can ever have such knowledge. The idealist responds: why insist that something is possible if it can never be actual? Far better to simply admit that nothing exists unless it exists inside a self. Of course, the sceptic would be entitled to respond: we cannot be certain that there is no reality any more than we can be certain that reality exists. In the end, the sceptic and the idealist are hard to distinguish: each of them doubts the existence of reality; each of them insists that we know nothing of reality.

Scepticism and idealism are terms used in Western philosophy, but similar ideas are found in Eastern philosophy too. For instance, many Buddhists and Hindus believe that our everyday experience is a 'veil of deception'; they call this veil 'maya'. Like the trick played on us by the evil demon, maya is an illusion that makes us believe falsely that the world is real. But for Eastern philosophers this trick is neither an imagined scenario nor evil. Rather, maya explains how our universe came to exist. The source of the universe – whoever or whatever that may be – plays a sort of cosmic game of hide-and-seek, by creating a veil of deception and then hiding behind it.

In Eastern as in Western philosophy, there is a blurry line between scepticism and idealism. If we exist on the wrong side of a veil of deception, we will never experience anything truly real, so we might as well go the whole hog and say that reality only exists in the mind. The *Diamond Sutra*, an ancient Buddhist text, concludes as much, in beautiful lines of verse:

*Thus shall ye think of this fleeting world:*
*A star at dawn, a bubble in a stream*
*A flash of lightening in a summer cloud*
*A flickering lamp, a phantom, and a dream.*

Scepticism and idealism are manifestations of an extreme form of self-absorption – *existential self-absorption*, it could be called. Existential self-absorption is a symptom of existential anxiety, a symptom of fearing being here now. A person with existential self-absorption attempts to deal with existential anxiety by hiding inside his self; if you dwell obsessively on the fact of your uncertainty, then reality seems to lose reality, in which case your uncertainty supposedly doesn't matter anymore. There's nothing to be uncertain about; all that remains is you and your perspective. Philosophers who hide in themselves advocate what I have called a 'one-sided' theory of human existence. Scepticism and idealism are one-sided theories, because if either of them is correct, then you are *not* here now; *you* exist but the world does not; the world collapses into your self, into a heap of guesses, or of waking dreams.

You don't have to be a philosopher to show signs of existential self-absorption. Many people go through phases of doubting everything. Philosophers are simply more persistent in their universal doubt than the rest of us. I don't know why many philosophers become self-absorbed to such an extreme degree. I don't even know why it happened to me. Still, in that furnace of fear and doubt, I learned lessons that, I hope, can help other people come to terms with uncertainty.

There is a way to overcome existential self-absorption, to shake off scepticism and idealism, to get back in touch with reality. There is a way we can use our uncertainty as a springboard from which we can regain confidence in our surroundings. And mindfulness can help, by inspiring us to be calm in the face of reality and curious in the face of uncertainty.

## Come Back to What You Know

If you ask your spouse or partner if they still love you, and they reply 'yes and no', it's fair to say they have some explaining to do. Well, the Small Answer to the Big Question of whether we really know anything is … yes and no. Obviously, I've got some explaining to do.

One of the reasons people get bogged down in mental distress is that, in a way, they are comforted by their distress. Consider an agoraphobic who is too frightened to leave the house. He is terrified of the outside world, but at the same time he finds his fear reassuring, because, so long as he is too terrified to face up to the world, he won't.

Similarly, a person suffering from existential self-absorption is afraid of reality, but is reassured by the thought that, so long as he remains mired in uncertainty, there will – supposedly – be no reality for him to face up to.

People with existential self-absorption need to be persuaded to accept reality. Simultaneously, they need to be persuaded to accept their uncertainty in the face of reality; otherwise, each time their uncertainty gets the better of them, they'll flee reality again. One of the ironies of accepting reality is that you must also accept the reality of uncertainty.

How can uncertainty and reality go together? It's time to revisit the model brain we made in chapter two. The model showed how human existence has a selfside and a worldside. As you flip the model over in your hands, you can see how each side recedes behind the prominence of the other. The selfside of your existence is where uncertainty resides; the world is uncertain from your point of view. When your self is prominent the world recedes behind your uncertainty; you are no longer simply experiencing the world; you are experiencing your perspective on the world, a perspective that may or may not be accurate. Yet, at the same time, the world doesn't go anywhere when it recedes behind your uncertainty. The world stays right there – *there*, you can *see* it: your perspective is a perspective on the world. The world – reality – is an integral part of your uncertainty, and vice versa.

To see that this analogy is correct, we need to show that reality does indeed lurk recessively behind uncertainty. Some of the most useful arguments in philosophy show this. They proceed one upon another, like a series of stepping stones back to reality.

Here's the first step: a person who claims that he knows nothing of reality must know at least one thing; he knows that he knows nothing. Admittedly, that's not a lot of knowledge, but it's a start. We've found a sliver of reality within existential self-absorption.

The second step revisits Descartes. Even if all your beliefs were false, at least one real entity would exist, namely, the believer of your beliefs, i.e. your self. Descartes favoured a two-placed theory of existence: he thought the self is a 'mental substance' that exists in a separate realm from reality. But surely he can't be right. You can't build a self out of the same ethereal mental states that the self is supposed to underpin. Moreover, a self that exists in a separate realm would be unable to affect reality. No, your self must be fully real. The obvious candidate for a real self is your brain, because if you switch your brain off, you switch off your mental life. So, reality – the museum of objects – contains at least one exhibit, namely, your brain.

The third step is a psychological observation about people with existential self-absorption. These people wouldn't claim to know nothing of reality unless they knew, deep down, that reality exists. Their knowledge of reality combined with their uncertainty is precisely what frightens them into hiding in uncertainty. The philosopher David Hume came up with a clever way of demonstrating that even the most existentially self-absorbed person is not being entirely honest with himself. If you ask such a person to do something dangerous, such as leaving a building by an upper-storey window rather than by the stairs, he will inevitably refuse, which will show that he knows very well that reality exists.

The fourth step is a subtle but ingenious observation made by the twentieth-century philosopher Donald Davidson. 'We may go plenty wrong', he notes, 'but only on condition that in most respects we are right'. Davidson's point is that our false beliefs can only be false if they *mean* something; a belief is false if its meaning describes incorrectly how the world is. But beliefs would lose all meaning unless they were flanked by a network of true beliefs. Suppose I mistakenly believe that a telegraph pole has fallen in a storm. Unless I have lots of true beliefs about telegraph poles and falling and storms, there's no way that my belief could be *about* anything; my belief would merely be nonsense. In turn, for my belief to mean something I'd also need to have lots of true beliefs about entities related to telegraph poles and falling and storms, say, electricity, gravity and wind, with further true beliefs related to those entities, and so on. Even if I have a belief about a non-existent entity, such as the Loch Ness Monster, the belief would be meaningless unless I had lots of suitable true beliefs, say, about Scotland and lochs and creatures that live underwater, and so on.

The sufferer of existential self-absorption makes a logical error. He assumes that because each of our beliefs could be false, all our beliefs could be false. They couldn't. Here's an equivalent error: each person who enters a lottery could win it, hence all the entrants could win it. They couldn't. Evil demons and veils of deception are out of the question if all our beliefs cannot be false. Reality avenges sceptics and idealists.

The fifth – and final – step is to let reality speak for itself, as it were. The philosopher G.E. Moore once gave a simple, common-sense refutation of scepticism. Raising his right hand, he said 'here is one hand', then, raising his left hand, he said 'here is another'. Moore's aim was to jolt his audience into paying attention to the obvious existence of reality. What, indeed, could be a more convincing proof that reality exists than to showcase reality itself?

Another Western philosopher who has adopted this 'showing' strategy is Jean-Paul Sartre. In an exhilarating passage in Sartre's novel *Nausea*, the narrator has an epiphany while staring at a tree root in a park. He suddenly realises that reality – 'existence' – is self-evident. He explains: 'all of a sudden, there it was, clear as day: existence had suddenly unveiled itself. It had lost the harmless look of an abstract category: it was the very paste of things, this root was kneaded into existence.'

Elsewhere, Sartre insists that the existence of the world is as obvious as the existence of the self. Alluding to Descartes's maxim 'I think therefore I am', Sartre says of reality, 'we can no more doubt it than we can doubt the I think'.

Eastern philosophy contains a special term for the indubitability of reality. The term is 'thatness', the idea being that we can conclusively demonstrate the existence of reality by saying 'Look at *that*', in the same way that we might draw a person's attention to a specific object or scene. In his book *The Way of Zen*, Alan Watts beguilingly suggests that 'thatness' is the first thing human beings ever notice about reality. When babies start to become aware of being alive, they point and say 'da'. We think they're pointing to daddy, says Watts, but actually they're pointing to *that* – to reality itself.

If 'thatness' sounds to you like a highbrow way of stating the bleeding obvious, you'd be right. Alas, intelligent people often have a habit of ignoring the bleeding obvious. Against such flakiness, the essayist Samuel 'Dr' Johnson – perhaps the greatest-ever doyen of common sense – often had stern words. His biographer, James Boswell, describes what happened when he confessed to Johnson that he didn't know how to refute idealism: 'I never shall forget the alacrity with which Johnson answered, striking his foot with mighty force against a large stone, till he rebounded from it – "I refute it thus".'

In pointing out that we can kick reality, Johnson was also reminding Boswell that reality kicks back. We don't always get our own way in life. We can't simply imagine or wish something would happen and – hey presto – it happens. Reality messes up our plans; we must deal with reality whether we like it or not; reality imposes itself upon us. Perhaps Boswell was lucky Johnson didn't make the point by slapping him across the face, a trick used by some Buddhist monks to alert their students to the existence of reality.

Reality imposes itself upon us not only in the practical sense, but also in the sense of the world just *being there*. No matter how many times you close your eyes and wish the world away, it won't budge. You open your eyes and *there it is*, imposing itself relentlessly upon your awareness.

When you consider the inevitability of imposition, the combination of reality and uncertainty seems entirely natural. If the world exists on its own terms, utterly independent of our dreams and schemes, then how can we expect, with our puny minds, to be certain about every aspect of reality? Faced with this realisation, the sensible response is not to retreat into uncertainty, but to accept that uncertainty and reality are two sides of our existence. Individually our beliefs might be false (the uncertainty side), but not all of them together (the reality side). Reality is indubitably there, imposing itself upon us, precisely insofar as it confounds our knowing.

## The Tree Root Meditation

If it were easy to face up to reality – a reality whose imposition upon us leaves us confounded and uncertain – no one would ever retreat into existential self-absorption. But facing up to reality isn't easy. Sartre's book is called *Nausea* because the tree root, the surrounding park, all of existence, gave the narrator (Sartre's mouthpiece) a sense of 'deep uneasiness'. To him, the root was 'rotten filth', 'a wooden serpent', 'entirely beastly'. All around him were 'monstrous masses' of existence, in their 'frightful, obscene nakedness'.

Sartre was frightened because he realised that the world couldn't be fully tamed by his knowledge. In the face of all those monstrous masses of reality, he understood he would always remain subordinate and uncertain. Robbed of his 'feeling of comfort and security', he felt 'crushed'; 'I hated this ignoble mess', he exclaims; 'I choked with rage'; 'it left me breathless'.

If only Sartre had tried mindfulness! By quietly meditating on his experience, breathing calmly all the while, he might have felt better about the existence of the tree root, the park, and indeed the whole world. He might even have felt pleased to exist. Despite its angst-ridden tone, Sartre's account of his visit to the park is suffused with a faint sense of exhilaration; at one point he openly admits to the 'atrocious joy' of the experience. Without the nausea, he might have felt only the joy.

In homage to Sartre, let's meditate on the naked existence of a tree root – but let's do it right.

Seek out the nearest tree – in your garden, a park, a forest, wherever. Sit down beside the tree, set your timer to ten minutes, then focus your attention on where the tree protrudes from the ground. Most likely, you've never closely observed a tree root before.

As you study the root, try to take in its details. Is it knotty? Smooth? Covered in bark, moss or fungus? Are any insects crawling on it? Is it grey, brown, black, green, white, orange, even blue? Is the surface reflective, or dull like an old pair of shoes? Is it dry, or studded with beads of water? So many details, overflowing – too many to take in!

As you study the root, take long, deep breaths. Calmly ignore any thoughts or emotions that flash through your psyche. Keep focusing on the root, as though its 'thatness' is holding your attention like a magnet. In these quiet, unreflective moments, while you sit calmly and in self-awareness beside this little piece of reality, you might learn to know reality for what it is – not what you wished it was, or feared it was, but what it is.

In mindfulness, you keep reality company like a loyal friend; you discover that you don't have to master the world to accept it.

## Mindful Uncertainty

In meditation we calmly and deliberately pay attention to our existence, and, in so doing, we learn to accept the imposition of reality upon our self-aware awareness.

Not everyone who meditates agrees with me on this. Some meditators think that in meditation we learn that the world is a veil of deception, that we are only aware of our selves. These life-denying meditators give up on the world – there's no point taking seriously something that's fake – and examine themselves instead. I've got nothing against self-examination, but, when it is performed as a means of deliberately ignoring reality, self-examination becomes existential self-absorption. In chapter five, we'll look in more detail at the imaginary menagerie of weird and wonderful entities that life-denying meditators perceive inside themselves.

For now, let's simply notice one fact: meditating on (or philosophising about) the so-called illusoriness of reality backfires. Fixating on a veil of deception doesn't make the illusion any less insistent. On the contrary, the sense of illusion is intensified, with the result that one's sense of uncertainty is intensified. If you're afraid of uncertainty, then rummaging around in your own mind looking for an antidote makes you feel more anxious than ever, in the long run.

Sometimes people say they are going on a meditation 'retreat'. What they mean by this depends on their attitude. Some see meditation as a way of retreating from the hurly-burly of life towards a vantage point from which they can see that reality is unreal. These meditators retreat from reality.

Other meditators, such as myself, see meditation differently. Through meditating we retreat from the hurly-burly of life, yes, but, during this temporary disengagement, our awareness of the world is heightened, as though we're taking stock, regrouping. We perceive reality *more* acutely, not less, when we calmly observe our experience under the spotlight of meditation. Indeed, the whole *point* of meditation is to try to see *beyond* – not *into* – the various thoughts and imaginings that comprise our inner lives. We retreat into meditation to become, in other words, more mindful of reality, as opposed to retreating into ourselves.

Through helping us to face up to reality, mindfulness also helps us to deal with reality. Through our self-aware awareness we soon become more confident in our surroundings; we build confidence *out of* uncertainty. That may sound counterintuitive, but confidence doesn't require certainty, only uncertainty harnessed correctly.

For example, we can develop confidence through learning. The foundation of learning is curiosity, and the engine of curiosity is uncertainty; when we are curious we pay close attention to the world, because we are eager to take in new information. Meditation is a great way of deliberately cultivating curiosity. By encouraging us to pitch our uncertainty against reality, mindfulness smoothly converts our uncertainty into curiosity. Meanwhile, the uncertainty that underlies our curiosity prevents our receptivity from slipping into naivety; uncertainty encourages us to criticise what we see and hear, to discover how things really are, not just how they seem to be.

Not all forms of attention qualify as curiosity. Consider what happens when you feel anxious due to uncertainty. Your attention zips around like a wasp, darting rapidly and haphazardly from one thing to another; you can't see the wood for the trees, and you can hardly see the trees either. By contrast, consider what happens in mindfulness, when you calmly accept your uncertainty: your focus is steadier – enabling you to access information less superficially – and your peripheral awareness is heightened too. Think of your attention as being like the sights of a gun. The crosshairs of the sights are analogous to the centre of your attention; the rings around the crosshairs are analogous to your peripheral attention. In mindfulness, the crosshairs of your attention stay relatively steady, which means that the rings of your attention stay steady too: you take in the details *and* the bigger picture. This coupling, which is optimal for information-gathering, is the hallmark of curiosity, and of learning.

Another – complementary – way to develop confidence is through engaging practically with the world. In teaching us to be self-aware and aware of imposition, mindfulness also reminds us – conversely – to impose ourselves upon reality. Wishing that the world would change is not enough: we must make it change, with our plans and our hands. The more we engage practically with the world, the more proficient we become at living, the more the world bends to our schemes, and the more confident we feel.

Learning begins with calmness but also enhances calmness. Psychologists talk about the 'hot' and 'cold' systems through which we react to our surroundings. The hot system encompasses our emotions and swift judgements; the cold system is how we rationally, dispassionately understand how the world works. Mercifully, the cold system subdues the hot system. So, a great way to dampen our anxiety is to cultivate a rational understanding of what we are afraid of. Sometimes, in doing so, we'll discover that our fear is reasonable. More often than not, we'll discover that it isn't.

**"The more we engage practically with the world, the more proficient we become at living"**

When you think about it, this entire book is an exercise in converting (hot) existential anxiety into a (cold) rational analysis of human existence. Through this analysis, I hope to convince you that you needn't be afraid of your existence. But within this broader project we can also use rational analysis to challenge some of our specific fears about uncertainty.

Consider terrorism. Many commentators have pointed out that people tend to overestimate their chances of being a victim of a terrorist attack. In his recent book *Thinking, Fast and Slow*, Daniel Kahneman noted that '[e]ven in countries that have been targets of intensive terror campaigns, such as Israel, the weekly number of casualties almost never came close to the number of traffic deaths'. Don't get me wrong: I'm not saying we shouldn't try to defeat terrorists, nor make reasonable adjustments in the face of the threat. The point is: rational analysis can help us to put into perspective the uncertainty that terrorism creates. For example, as I write, some commentators have recently suggested that since 11 September 2001 Americans have had as much chance of being killed by *their own furniture* as by a terrorist attack on US soil. And history tells us that most terrorist groups have ended up failing to achieve their strategic goals.

Rationality takes some of the sting out of many of the scares peddled by the media. Globally, our chances of dying in an extreme weather event have never been lower. Wars have never been rarer. Our lives are safer, healthier and longer than ever, especially – but not only – in the West. Don't take my word for it. Authors such as Matt Ridley (in *The Rational Optimist*) and Steven Pinker (in *The Better Angels of Our Nature*) have meticulously documented the unprecedented peacefulness and prosperity of our modern era.

I'm not suggesting we should be arrogant or complacent, or that we should be falsely confident, puffed up by delusional optimism. Far from it. Mindfulness, by encouraging us to face up to uncertainty and reality, also encourages us to be prudent. But prudence itself leads to confidence. The knowledge that we've taken precautions is a bridge from uncertainty to confidence.

Through learning, practicality, rationality and prudence we can increase the predictability and dependability of our everyday surroundings. How, indeed, could it be otherwise? If we give up engaging with reality, shocked into submission like the morose dogs in Seligman and Maier's study, the only thing we can be confident about is that there will be future shocks we could have avoided but didn't. We can maximise our confidence only by using our uncertainty; by finding out more about what we're dealing with; by analysing situations rationally rather than reacting to them in an emotional or intuitive way; and by taking steps to make sure we can prevent as many potential problems as possible, or cope with those problems should they arise. We might not necessarily be able to prevent our spouse from leaving, or the car from breaking down, or the alarm clock from malfunctioning, or our boss from firing us, or the rope from snapping, but at least we can equip ourselves to deal with such eventualities, thus preventing them from snowballing individually, or accumulating collectively, to form a crisis.

Turning uncertainty into confidence often means learning from the experts; you can't work it all out on your own. But we can also develop confidence through our everyday social relationships. A commitment to dealing with reality leads naturally to co-operative relationships with the people around us – with our families, partners, friends and communities. When we can trust and depend on our fellows, we grow in confidence. Moreover, when we support each other in our lives – when we deal with reality together, through face-to-face, practical social interactions – we forgo the dubious 'shared' experiences offered up by television and the internet; we raise our voices above the confidence-shattering siren songs of the marketers and broadcasters and politicians; and we marginalise bureaucrats with their arbitrary and unsettling intrusions into our affairs.

Next time you feel uncertain, pause. Then breathe. Then focus on your surroundings. Once you've established that you're not in clear and present danger, simply ignore the knee-jerk fears and doubts and catastrophic visions that flash through your psyche. Recover your composure. Talk to someone trustworthy about what you're worried about. Find out what the experts say about what you fear. Perform your own investigations. Turn your uncertainty into curiosity, into learning. Enhance your sense of calm, through reasoning and understanding and prudence. Take stock to take control, to avoid slipping into learned helplessness and derealisation, into self-absorption, into that vicious circle in which a chronic fear of uncertainty fuels a chronic fear of uncertainty. Be mindful.

Even when our powers of comprehension and prediction utterly fail us, mindfulness can still help us, because, after all, mindfulness teaches us to come to terms with the inevitability of uncertainty in the face of reality. Will a devastating new disease emerge from the swamps of the Earth and wipe out humanity in a generation? Will aliens arrive from outer space and swat us aside with their superior technologies? Who knows? In the East and West, philosophers throughout the ages have independently discovered a gentle but powerful mood that soothes intractable ignorance: fatalism. This mood is captured in the popular saying: *que sera sera* (whatever will be, will be). In cases where you truly cannot mitigate your uncertainty, why worry? You might as well accept your fate, whatever it may be, and enjoy the here and now in the meantime.

..........................................

# Four

# Am I Free?

Reality can be overwhelming. It can make us feel out of control of our destiny, tossed this way and that, like the proverbial cork upon the tide. And our burden of responsibility for our choices can make us feel no less overwhelmed. When we feel unable to cope, we sometimes find consolation in fate, in accepting 'que sera sera'. But for some people, fate becomes a way of life. These disconsolate souls give up trying to influence their future. Resigning themselves to whatever life holds in store for them, they renounce their individuality and their freedom; they abandon themselves to reality, surrender to what they can't fully control. In doing so, they compound one impossible quest with another. Far better to be mindful of freedom — and freer through mindfulness.

I s it good or bad to be on your own? The verdict of popular culture on this question is strangely ambivalent. For every song, book or film about the pain of loneliness, isolation, rejection and alienation, there's another about the glory of solitude, uniqueness, independence and freedom. Whether being on your own is a good thing or not is a matter of perspective, it seems. You have to decide.

Of course, in this sense, each of us is as alone as can be. Your perspective is yours alone, because the selfside of your existence is for you only. No one else will ever be you; they'll never know first-hand what goes on inside your self. This special – existential – kind of aloneness can never be masked by the quality of your relationships. Other people can join you, yet they cannot reach you. The burden of being you is yours to bear alone.

And what a burden it is! On the one hand, there is the entire universe; on the other hand, there is you. It is not much of an exaggeration to say that you bear the weight of the world upon your shoulders. The relentless imposition of reality on your awareness means that you cannot escape the pressure of existing; instead you must choose how to react to that pressure.

No wonder we all find the burden hard to bear sometimes. No wonder we sometimes seek to divest ourselves of it. We can't give ourselves away – that's precisely the problem – so we try to shed the burden through trying to escape from ourselves. No more me, no more burden, we tell ourselves.

We get out of our heads, out of our minds, off our faces, off our trees, off our rockers. We fly off the handle, go ape, blow our tops, blow our stacks, go off the deep end. We go with the flow, let ourselves go, cut loose, let the handbrake off, lose control, lose ourselves. Eskimos, it is often remarked, have fifty words for snow, a fact that reflects the importance of snow in their lives. Similarly, the many phrases or paraphrases we have for losing ourselves reflects the importance of this activity in our lives.

If you're someone who likes to lose yourself – if you're someone who takes a negative perspective on having a perspective – then bear this in mind: you can change your perspective. You can embrace your existential aloneness instead of fearing it and hiding from it. You can bear the burden of being you, with pride.

I often think of this when I listen to 'Like a Rolling Stone' by Bob Dylan. One of my favourite songs, it's an epic story of a rich socialite's decline into penury and isolation. In the song's legendary chorus, Dylan asks his protagonist how it *feeeeeels* to be alone. When you first hear this lyric, it sounds like a vindictive snarl, a rubbing of salt into the wound of the protagonist's sudden aloneness. Yet, as you listen, you cannot help but notice that there is euphoria in Dylan's voice, too. As you sing along with him, Dylan's grinning rhetorical question becomes less of a taunt and more of an empathetic nod to the protagonist's new-found liberation: the song is transformed into a stirring paean to individuality and freedom.

This chapter is about how it feels to be alone. It is about how philosophers have encouraged us to lose ourselves in the face of reality, but how we can learn to reassert and celebrate our individuality and our freedom. It is about how mindfulness teaches us to keep ourselves, not lose ourselves, but also teaches us to loosen ourselves; to act naturally without letting ourselves go. A rolling stone, after all, rolls.

## The Real Rumble

For most people with existential anxiety, being told that uncertainty is nothing to worry about because reality imposes itself relentlessly upon us doesn't immediately sound like much of a consolation.

Nor does it help much to hear that reality is an equal opportunity imposer. We are not, as it turns out, the only ones upon whom reality imposes itself. Everyone and every*thing* gets imposed upon by other real things. Reality imposes itself upon reality.

The nineteenth-century German philosopher Arthur Schopenhauer gained a reputation as the most depressing thinker in history for pointing out reality's strange animus against itself. Looking out upon the world, Schopenhauer saw a vast battle of wills. Every object, he declared, contains an inner essence, and this essence is a blind striving, surging, willing. Each object is pitted against each other, in a never-ending battle for existence itself; a sort of existential wrestling match of all against all – a 'Real Rumble', you might say. The rain hammers against the mountainside. The sun melts the ice. The lion devours the lamb. The stray ball smashes the windowpane. The bomb destroys the town.

Schopenhauer was one of the first Western philosophers to be influenced by Hinduism and Buddhism. For thousands of years, Eastern philosophers had emphasised that everything that exists is fragile, prone to disintegration, impermanent. It is said that the Buddha's last words were: 'Decay is inherent in all compounded things; strive on with diligence.' Schopenhauer added an extra layer of dismalness to this cataclysmic vision: everything decays because all things impose themselves upon other things, inevitably grinding everything to dust.

This view of reality may sound somewhat adolescent, but the idea of a Real Rumble is inherent to the world views of two of the greatest scientists in history.

Albert Einstein saw imposition everywhere. His special theory of relativity proved that mass and energy are 'interchangeable' – in effect, the same thing. To exist as an object basically means to have a mass; so, all objects are equivalent to the energy they contain. When objects interact, they transfer energy to each other; this is called exerting a force. So – putting Einstein's insight metaphorically – we can say that the whole universe is a theatre of conflict in which objects continually exert forces upon each other.

Half a century before Einstein, Charles Darwin noticed the ubiquity – and the consequences – of imposition in the natural world. Species survive from generation to generation, Darwin realised, only if they successfully resist destruction. Each species is adapted in various ways to its surroundings; through these adaptations, the ancestors of each species imposed themselves upon reality, and, in turn, resisted being fatally imposed upon. Nature, in this way, 'selects' well-adapted organisms, and, over time, each species gradually accumulates in its make-up any useful new adaptations that have arisen through random mutations in individual organisms: in other words, species 'evolve'. What makes nature 'horribly cruel', as Darwin put it, is that most organisms can only survive by way of an extreme form of imposition: consuming other organisms. The raw material that makes life possible is like real estate; there's a limited amount of it. Organisms must commandeer enough of that material to exist, and other organisms are indispensable sources of it.

Darwin's contemporaries were disturbed by his theory of evolution. They were especially freaked out by his suggestion that human beings evolved through natural selection. Like it or not, Darwin was proven right. Encoded in our genes and instincts are many of the very same adaptations that enabled our ape-like ancestors to survive and reproduce.

Combining Einstein's and Darwin's insights, we can see that everything that exists is doubly influenced by forces. On one hand, each object (including each species) is dictated to by the forces of the objects surrounding it; objects are imposed upon. On the other hand, each object is dictated to by forces within itself. To exist, each object must emerge out of the past, unbowed and unbroken, still standing despite everything that has been thrown at it. In turn, each object is propelled futurewards, launched on to its present surroundings, by the very same inner forces that propelled it through the maelstrom of the past. Imposition is the residue of survival.

The contents of our minds are inner forces that launch us on to our surroundings. Many of these psychological forces are no different from those that successfully launched our ancestors out of the past. Many, and perhaps all, of the emotions and feelings we experience today helped our ancestors respond vigorously to threats and opportunities. Many of our modern judgements, too – about what is good, what is bad, what is lovely, what is foul – recapitulate our ancestors' successful strategies for surviving and reproducing. And our suffering – our pain, hunger, fear, and so on – reflects how our ancestors dealt with trouble, how they were inwardly pushed into behaviour that would maximise their chances of living to fight – or love – another day.

Sadly, imposition is exquisitely suited to making us suffer. The main sources of suffering in life – pain, loss and death – are all consequences of the Real Rumble. Pain is how our nervous systems desperately try to respond to bodily disintegration, whether from injury, invasion or ageing. Loss – of property, and, infinitely worse, of loved ones – is inevitable in a world where impermanence is woven into the fabric of everything. Imposition ensures that death is everyone's fate.

And, perhaps worst of all, we must endure these, and every other form of imposition, on our own. Our emotions and feelings surge up into our lonely minds like hot geysers out of desert sands. Our thoughts surround us like a swarm of insistent insects. Our suffering waltzes in uninvited to the most private of sanctums. The inner forces that dictate to us are impersonal and indifferent, yet up close and personal. And, all the while, the outside world comes at us like waves pounding against the shores of our selves.

No wonder people try to escape themselves. No wonder, indeed, some people have made an art form out of self-escape. Let's get to know these self-escape artists, otherwise known as philosophers.

## How to Argue Yourself Unconscious

For thousands of years philosophers have been asking, in one way or another, 'what is consciousness?'. They might have made a bit more progress if they'd asked Louis Armstrong.

'If you gotta ask, you ain't never gonna get to know' was how Armstrong replied when he was asked by a journalist what jazz is. Armstrong's point was that jazz is fundamentally something that must be *experienced* to be understood. If you're asking callow questions about jazz, presumably you haven't personally experienced it, and you're never going to experience it through asking questions.

The same is true of human consciousness. If someone said to you, 'I've no idea what human consciousness is. Can you tell me about it?' the question would sound strange – alarming, even. You'd be inclined to respond, 'Aren't you *already* conscious? If you're not, you're never going to understand consciousness through asking about it'.

In other words, human consciousness – of the world, of our bodies, of our emotions and feelings and thoughts and imaginings – cannot be understood without direct personal experience. You've got to experience being conscious to know what consciousness is. Accordingly, consciousness can only be fully understood by an *experiencer*, by a self with a private inner viewpoint, by an individual person for whom personal experience happens.

I wrote '*fully* understood' because there are some aspects to your experience that could be understood by an enquirer who was totally ignorant about consciousness.

The enquirer could study your brain and nervous system to find out more about visual, auditory, olfactory and gustatory processing; about the physiology of emotions and feelings and other bodily sensations; and about how and where thoughts and mental images arise from neurons in your brain. But in all of this, the enquirer would never encounter *you*. No matter how much detail he uncovered about your brain, and about its links to your body, he'd never know anything about *being* your brain, about being you. With no personal experience of his own, he'd remain ignorant about the essential, private aspect of consciousness, the aspect without which there wouldn't be any such thing as consciousness at all.

However, for some philosophers, the self's elusiveness points to a radically different conclusion. If no self can be discovered through studying the brain of a conscious person, these philosophers say, then the brain of a conscious person doesn't contain a self; consciousness doesn't require personal experience. Being conscious, so it goes, involves nothing more than all the relevant neurological processes that could be studied by an enquirer who was totally ignorant about consciousness. Once the enquirer had fully understood how your nervous system works, he'd know everything there is to know about your experience.

Philosophers who believe that consciousness is solely a neurological process are called 'materialists'. Materialism is another example of a one-sided theory of human existence. According to materialists, your self doesn't really exist. Your consciousness is nothing more than your brain and nervous system; your experience is nothing more than the various inner and outer forces that shape your brain's interactions with the world.

The worldside of your existence exists, but not the selfside; consciousness is nothing more than matter.

Materialists are savvy enough to realise that their theory is unlikely to win approval unless they explain why most non-philosophers (and some philosophers) believe in the existence of the self; after all, most people will be reluctant to relinquish their individuality without understanding why they've been so radically mistaken about themselves. How, then, do materialists explain why so many of us persistently believe we have a private, inner view of the world?

Some materialists say, dismissively, that we're simply clinging to a primitive, outdated belief, as though we still believed that the Earth is flat, or that fairies exist. Other materialists say, more charitably, that the self is an extremely convincing illusion conjured up by the brain; just as the sun and the rain combine to form a rainbow, the various material aspects of your consciousness – i.e. the parts of your brain that underlie your feelings, sensations, thoughts, and so on – combine to form the illusion that is you.

Some materialists add – with some irony – that we can establish that the self is unreal simply by using our own minds to seek ourselves. David Hume noted that when we look inwards we encounter lots of experiences but not an *experiencer*. He concluded that the self doesn't exist; it is merely a 'bundle' of experiences – just as a rainbow is a bundle of raindrops and light.

Bob Dylan would not approve. When philosophers argue about the existence of the self, there is more at stake than whether or not we have a private, inner perspective on the world. The existence of such a perspective is, more importantly, a precondition of our *freedom*. You cannot be free if *you* don't exist (and, indeed, if you do exist then you are free). If you are nothing more than a bundle of experiences, you're no more in control of your life than, say, a cat in a washing machine.

Among materialists there is an ongoing debate about human freedom. On one side are the 'determinists'. According to determinism, everything that happens in the universe is fixed in advance – 'determined' – by the laws of nature. This means that if we could reset the universe back to the Big Bang, and press play again, whatever happened the first time would happen exactly the same the second time, and the third time, and so on.

Other materialists are 'indeterminists'; they argue that everything that happens *isn't* determined in advance. To support this view, these materialists often argue that reality is governed by probabilities, as though the universe must roll a dice at every instant to establish what happens next (this is a view based on modern physics, which has found that subatomic particles seem to be governed by chance). If we could replay a probabilistic universe from the start, things would turn out differently every time.

When it comes to human freedom, the materialists' debate about determinism and indeterminism is a red herring. If you don't exist, if you don't have a self, then you don't have any freedom, regardless of whether the universe is probabilistic or not.

Some materialists miss this point. They think that if reality rolls a dice to decide what human beings do next, this would be a kind of freedom. It wouldn't. Freedom doesn't mean acting by chance. If it did, we'd be no more free than anything else that exists in a probabilistic universe – say, a meteor or a dung beetle. Our lives would be fully controlled by inner and outer forces, even if some of these forces were random. Freedom means acting by choice, not by chance.

Nonetheless, if you *are* free then indeterminism is correct. A universe that contains freedom will turn out differently every time; our choices are not fixed in advance by the laws of nature. But a universe that turns out differently every time won't necessarily contain freedom. Materialists who are indeterminists are right about indeterminism, but they are wrong about freedom.

Some philosophers insist that we can make choices even if we're not free. Schopenhauer claimed (and Einstein agreed with him) that 'man can do what he wills but he cannot will what he wills', while Hume, similarly, was a 'compatibilist' who argued that making choices is compatible with determinism. Clearly, this is absurd – like arguing that you can be dead and alive at the same time. You can't make a choice if you're not free to choose what you choose!

Materialism is a trendy philosophy these days in the West, especially among scientists. Lots of books have been published recently in which famous scientists deny the existence of the self and freedom – of *selfdom*, as we might call the combination. These authors might be surprised to hear that they are championing ideas that, in one form or another, go back as far as Buddhism and Hinduism.

Two and a half thousand years ago the Buddha claimed – in a similar manner to David Hume – that we cannot discover a self over and above the various forces that shape our inner and outer experiences. Moreover, the Buddha argued, you are different now from who you were in the past, and from who you will be in future, so there is no such entity as 'you' who abides through time. The self, accordingly, is an illusion. Buddhists portentously call this 'the doctrine of no-self'.

Most Hindus don't (exactly) believe in the self either. As we'll see in the next chapter, they believe (along with some Buddhists) that the individual self is actually part of a bigger, universal self. *You* don't really exist if you're inseparable from a universal self that belongs to everyone and everything else.

Strangely, there isn't much discussion of freedom among philosophers in the Eastern tradition. Perhaps they consider the matter closed if there's no such thing as an individual self. (And perhaps Buddhists are following the lead of the Buddha, who kept a 'noble silence' when asked whether determinism or indeterminism is true.)

However, in Buddhism and Hinduism there is an important doctrine that can be interpreted as a rejection of freedom. The 'doctrine of non-attachment' implores us to stop 'attaching' ourselves to various objects or people. We form these attachments because we hope that, through them, we will satisfy the desires of our self. But 'grasping' at reality in this way is pointless, say many Buddhists and Hindus; the individual self doesn't exist, so, through our attachments, we're trying to satisfy a non-existent entity – a hopeless task.

The doctrine of non-attachment is tied in with the theme of impermanence in Eastern philosophy. If every object and person must soon become non-existent, then our attempt to achieve satisfaction by grasping at reality is even more pointless.

To me, the doctrine of non-attachment sounds plainly like a rejection of freedom. We make choices because we want to preserve or bring about particular states of affairs in the world. When Eastern thinkers tell us that we don't really exist as selves, and that we shouldn't grasp at the world, they're dismissing everything it means to be free.

Some Buddhists and Hindus might argue that what 'non-attachment' really means is that our freedom creates a distance between ourselves and the various inner and outer forces that impact upon us; we shouldn't, so it goes, pretend to ourselves that our attachments to the world can ever make this distance disappear. Non-attachment, on this view, is just another word for the way in which mindfulness disentangles us from our experiences by creating a clearing in our minds. I entirely agree that this clearing, this distance, exists. However, this cannot always be what non-attachment means in the Eastern tradition, given the propensity of Buddhists and Hindus to deny the existence of the self. Without a self, the doctrine of non-attachment is all about the idea of not 'grasping' at reality. And this idea, like materialism, gives us no recourse or encouragement to resist our fate, to exercise our freedom, to reach across the span of our awareness and freely change the world.

All these various examples of denying the existence of selfdom could be described as *existential self-escape*. This extreme, and extremely persistent, attempt to lose oneself is a reaction to existential anxiety. Existential self-escapers, like all people with existential anxiety, fear being here now, but above all they fear their existential loneliness. They try to escape from existential loneliness by escaping forever from themselves. They, too, need to be persuaded to come back to what they know.

## Condemned to be Free

Steven Spielberg's film *Minority Report* contains one of my favourite ever scenes. The film is set in a future in which the police can detect and punish criminal acts before they happen. The main character, John Anderton, is a cop who works for the police's 'pre-crime' unit, aided by three mysterious 'pre-cogs', mutant humans who can see into the future. Motivated by the loss of his son, Sean, who was murdered before the pre-cogs were discovered, Anderton is an exemplary officer who believes passionately in his work. But one day, shockingly, the pre-cogs name him as a future murderer. He manages to escape, then goes on the run. Desperately searching for an explanation as to why he would ever commit murder, he stumbles upon a shady-looking man in a hotel room. Scattered around the man are various photographs of children, and, with a growing sense of horror, Anderton recognises his late son amongst them. The man confesses on the spot – somewhat zealously – to Sean's murder, and suddenly we realise, as viewers, the tragic fate that has been in store for Anderton all along. He draws his gun, his finger twitching on the trigger, his mind racing with memories of his son and of his estranged wife, his pain haunting him, his desire for revenge welling up, the prophecy of the pre-cogs coming to pass. And then something incredible happens.

Anderton doesn't shoot. He chooses not to. Defying the inner and outer forces that the pre-cogs (and, no doubt, every viewer) assumed would prevail, he arrests the man.

This wonderful scene symbolises the power of human freedom – the power of the self to choose. Yet the scene also symbolises the unworldliness of freedom's power. If we studied Anderton's brain and his surroundings, we'd be able to discover the various forces, inner and outer, that were arrayed against his innocence, but we'd never find the spark of freedom that defied his guilt. No doubt, we'd also find some worldly forces that motivated Anderton to do the right thing; for instance, presumably he wanted to be a good cop, and didn't want to be a killer. However, Spielberg's direction vividly conveys to us that, unassisted, Anderton's nobler motives couldn't have overridden the force of his desire to commit murder in that harrowing moment. The unworldly power of Anderton's freedom enabled him to choose which of his motivations to reinforce, and which thereby to convert into action.

Freedom's unworldly power is both obvious and undetectable. We can appreciate this strange dichotomy by looking inwards, too. David Hume was correct that the self is elusive, but he drew the wrong conclusion. The self exists all right, and freedom exists, even though you can't point at your selfdom and say 'there it is'. You are the selfside of your brain, the very opposite of your brain, so you won't find any *thing* to point at when you contemplate your self and your choices. You can *be* yourself, you can *make* choices – this much is obvious. But you wouldn't be you and you wouldn't be free if your choices were objects that you (or anyone else) could see.

At the same time, your choices must impact upon reality. The unification of the selfside and the worldside of your brain explains how your choices can affect the world. The selfside is an aspect of your brain, and your brain is a bundle of forces like any other object. Whatever your self chooses, these choices must manifest themselves amid the various forces that comprise your brain's worldside. Indeed, we can appreciate now why the self has freedom at all. Freedom is the force of the self, the self made real.

If we're going to coax existential self-escapers back to themselves and to freedom, we need to show them how to return from reality to the obvious existence of themselves – from the worldside to the selfside of their brains. The journey is the reverse of the one we made in chapter three, when we moved from uncertainty to reality. Freedom sits naturally alongside uncertainty in the selfside of our brains; both uncertainty and freedom create a 'distance' between ourselves and reality.

As we head back towards the self, we can see that the terrain is familiar. When people deny the existence of their self and their freedom they obviously do not believe they have any control over their lives. In this respect, existential self-escapers are similar to people who suffer from existential self-absorption. Extreme uncertainty, you will recall, begins with learned helplessness – a sense that one's surroundings have become so uncontrollable and unpredictable that one might as well give up. When learned helplessness is combined with derealisation, people often slide into a total denial that they know anything about reality.

Sometimes, however, learned helplessness is accompanied by another strange psychological state: 'depersonalisation'. When people feel out of control, they sometimes feel that they are losing a sense of their own agency. They may be overwhelmed by inner or outer forces, or both, but the result is the same. Depersonalisation makes people feel like a 'robot', or as though they're living on 'autopilot', in the words of some sufferers. Their sense of selfdom fades, because their efforts to influence their lives have proven futile. Existential self-escape is depersonalisation in an extreme form – a denial that personal agency is even possible.

A sense of lacking control over one's life is a knife-edge of discomfort from which people sometimes topple into total uncertainty and sometimes into a total surrender to reality. The relentless imposition of reality upon a person's awareness can make him feel completely uncertain, his self cut off from reality, or completely overwhelmed, his self dissolved by the forces of reality.

Like existential self-absorption, existential self-escape gives rise to a combination of comfort and fear. Though it is frightening to think that one has lost control over one's life, it is comforting to think that one never had a self all along, and therefore never had any control to lose. Escaping yourself is, supposedly, a way to escape the anxiety and frustrations that go along with being a self. As long as your selfdom doesn't exist, you'll never have to face up to the terror of being you.

Selfdom is frightening when we feel out of control, but being in control can be just as frightening. Being free means having responsibility for our choices. Whatever we choose, we could have chosen otherwise; we are not forced to choose one thing over another. In turn, we are responsible for the consequences of our choices, especially when those consequences were predictable. Responsibility can be unnerving. Being responsible can mean having to accept guilt or blame. The thought of being held accountable by others (and by ourselves) can make us scared of our selfdom.

Of course, in any particular situation the extent of our freedom and therefore our responsibility varies according to the extent of our abilities. For instance, if you don't know how to fly a plane, you're not free to safely land a jumbo jet after the pilot passes out. You are always free to choose – but you can't choose to do something you simply can't do.

Sometimes we fear our selfdom not only because we fear the potential consequences of our choices, but because we fear the choices we might potentially make. Being free means that you cannot guarantee in advance what you will choose; this uncertainty can make you fear what you will freely do in the future. If you've ever stood at the edge of a cliff you'll know what I'm talking about. Many people in this situation step back from the edge, frightened by the realisation that they're free to throw themselves off (or, worse, push someone else off).

Philosophers call fear of freedom 'anguish'; if you don't have a self, you can't suffer anguish. Indeed, without a self you wouldn't suffer at all. The inner and outer forces that surge into your awareness would be irrelevant to you if you didn't exist. They'd be no more *your* problem than the problems of any other person or creature or object. Whether self-escapers fear their selfdom because they fear losing control, or because they fear being responsible, or because they fear what they might choose to do in future, or because they fear suffering, self-escape provides comfort insofar as, without a self, people supposedly will never have to face up to being themselves.

Yet the fear shown by self-escapers is a two-way street; it can also lead them back to themselves. The persistence of fear amid the comfort of self-escape indicates that self-escapers know very well that the self exists and freedom exists. If self-escapers *really* thought that they didn't have a self and that they weren't free, they wouldn't continue to fear being themselves.

When people know that the Loch Ness Monster doesn't exist, they stop being afraid of it; in contrast, people continue being afraid of things whose existence they're in denial about.

By recognising that their persistent fear of themselves is a fear of what they haven't truly escaped from, self-escapers can begin to acknowledge the existence of their selfdom. And they can begin to accept their selfdom by recognising that self-escape is not only futile, it *exacerbates* the problem of fearing oneself. If you're worried about losing control, the last thing you should do is deny that your selfdom exists; when we believe that we have no influence over our lives, we allow ourselves to be dominated by the inner and outer forces of our experience. Likewise, when we give up trying to act with responsibility, we become more, not less, compromised by the consequences of our actions – and we end up suffering more. And if you renounce your selfdom because you're afraid that you can't (yet) control your future choices, you give yourself even less control over your life; submitting to your impulses is hardly more likely to make you behave well than entrusting yourself to your own freedom.

Jean-Paul Sartre noted that when we deny our freedom we are actually making a choice: we are choosing to kid ourselves. He called our self-deceptive denial of freedom 'bad faith'. As an example of bad faith, Sartre describes a woman on a first date who freezes up when her suitor takes hold of her hand. Not confident enough to decide whether or not to resist the man's advances, the woman allows herself to believe that her hand is a mere 'thing' over which she has no control. Actually, in freely giving up her control of her hand, she *has* made a choice: she has chosen to lie to herself about her freedom. She has chosen to surrender to her circumstances.

Even in the most pressurised of circumstances, we remain free. Sartre cites the example of France under the Nazi occupation. At almost every moment, the French were faced with a choice of whether to resist or collaborate. Many people found that the occupation oddly intensified their awareness of their freedom, by forcing them to face up to the choice of how to respond to being oppressed; 'never were we freer than under the German occupation', Sartre surmised. From this crucible of war, he drew the famous, and inspiring, conclusion that 'man is condemned to be free': everywhere and always, people can make some sort of choice amid the constraints life places upon them.

Alas, the strategy of using fear to lure self-escapers back into themselves can backfire: after all, a fear of selfdom can also push people towards the comfort of existential self-escape. Is there, instead, a way to help people fearlessly face up to themselves?

Sometimes people can perceive errors more calmly in others than in themselves (that's why group therapy can be so effective). Imagine if somebody close to you was behaving foolishly – say, gambling all his money away, drinking beer all day long, or playing video games instead of getting a job. Now imagine if this person claimed to have no choice in how he was behaving. He might say he was so stressed, or addicted, or disillusioned, or angry, he couldn't help himself. How would you respond? I suspect, like me, you'd try to help him by alerting him to his sense of self, to his capacity to choose how to behave. The error of self-escape is obvious when someone else is committing it. Accordingly, people who try to escape from their selfdom might be persuaded to see the erroneousness of their views by reflecting on other people who hold the same dismal views.

Self-escapers can also be encouraged to reflect rationally on their own selfdom. From a rational point of view, the idea that we can be 'mistaken' about having a self, and the idea that the self is an 'illusion', makes no sense at all. If you're mistaken about being you, then who exactly is mistaken, if not you? And who experiences the illusion of being you, if not you? Moreover, if you weren't you in the past, and you won't be you in the future, then why do you still care what happens to you in the future? (Every self-escaper, if he's honest, does care; why else would he brush his teeth, for instance?) The self keeps popping up like a bump in the carpet every time self-escapers try to make themselves disappear.

Unfortunately, fear can all too readily overwhelm reason; that's precisely why self-escapers are so persistent in their irrationality. Wouldn't it be wonderful if we could somehow persuade these wretched souls to be calmly aware of their own freedom, calmly aware of their capacity to rise above their circumstances and emotions, calmly aware of their responsibility for their lives?

Wouldn't it be wonderful, indeed, if we could all be more mindful of our freedom?

## A Freedom Meditation

Mindfulness is a state of calm, self-aware awareness. When we meditate mindfully, breathing gently and deeply all the while, deliberately paying attention to ourselves and to our experience, we become highly aware of our own minds, and of our surroundings. Meditation, therefore, can help us learn to accept, without fear or regret, the existence of our selfdom amid the various inner and outer forces that comprise our awareness.

Some meditations encourage us to anchor our attention to specific aspects of our experience, say, our breathing, our bodies, a particular sensory experience, or a particular aspect of our surroundings. I'd like to invite you to meditate on the *inner experience of making a choice*. There are two aspects to making a choice: firstly, we choose where to direct our attention; secondly, we choose to act.

Let's get started by setting ourselves up to meditate, sitting up straight, with our hands resting on our thighs; on this occasion, however, keep your palms facing upwards. Begin your meditation by focusing on your breathing. Once you feel calm and alert, turn your attention to your hands. Deliberately move your attention from one finger to another, randomly, if you like – there doesn't have to be any particular pattern. The key word here is *deliberately*. Notice how your attention seamlessly responds to your momentary choices to move it. Normally our attention moves around automatically, but when you are in a state of mindfulness, the only thing forcing you to move your attention is the unworldly force of your freedom.

As you freely move your attention from one finger to another, I'd like you to choose whether or not to wiggle the finger upon which your attention is trained (if you like, you can imagine you're John Anderton with his finger on the trigger). Notice again that if you choose to wiggle a finger, the only thing forcing you to do so is your freedom.

As usual, try not to be distracted by any extraneous thoughts, sensations and feelings that pop into your awareness. Just notice all these inner flickerings, then gently bring your attention back to the task at hand (bad pun intended).

After ten minutes of this meditation I hope you'll have a vivid sense not only of who you are but also *what you can do*. You are the selfside of your existence, and you can freely influence this particular part of your body.

And, of course, that's just the start. Your fingers are exquisite tools that are designed to respond to your choices in many ways other than wiggling. Similarly, you can activate the myriad potentialities of the rest of your body by using your choices. In turn, you can use your hands and your body to freely influence the world beyond your body – the possibilities of your freedom are almost endless.

When we meditate on our freedom, we remind ourselves: I am here now, and I can choose what to do now.

## Mindful Freedom

In case you haven't worked it out by now, the answer is a resounding 'yes'! I'm talking, of course, about the Small Answer to the Big Question of whether or not you are free. You *are* free; we all are.

We are free insofar as, as individuals, we can choose what to pay attention to, and whether or not to initiate actions. The force via which we exercise these choices is evoked by our self-awareness. In self-awareness, our self becomes prominent as reality recedes. The self becomes an unworldly presence within the world, and therefore exerts an unworldly force: freedom. Yet even as this force emanates from ourselves, the self is an aspect of the brain; hence, the force of freedom affects the worldside of the brain. Our choices shape our brains and therefore instruct our bodies and therefore affect reality.

The prominence of the self creates a distance between us and the inner and outer forces that impose themselves upon our awareness. Across this distance, we can freely choose how we respond to those forces.

In mindfulness we deliberately cultivate a prominent self, in order to influence our lives consciously and freely. Advocates of mindfulness often emphasise the importance of distancing ourselves from our thoughts, sensations, feelings, emotions, imaginings, and so on. This emphasis is justified. Compared to the outer forces that surround us, inner forces have a disproportionate effect upon us; up close and personal, they are an ever-present filter through which our experiences and actions are modified.

Skilled meditators often encourage us to 'accept' the various thoughts, feelings, sensations and so on, that flit through our minds. Acceptance is important because it helps us to avoid being dictated to by our experiences. When we see a cloud in the sky, we simply acknowledge that 'there's a cloud' – we accept, in a cool and detached way, what we are seeing. Similarly, acceptance allows us to coolly acknowledge what we're thinking or feeling without necessarily acting on our impulses.

However, some critics of mindfulness have pointed out – rightly – that acceptance shouldn't mean acquiescence. If you treated your experiences exactly as you treat clouds, you'd never *do* or *change* anything; you'd just sit there passively gazing, like – well – a cloud-gazer. The whole point of acceptance is that, through disentangling ourselves from our experiences, we can create our own climate, as it were. By choosing which aspects of our inner lives to ignore and which to pay attention to, we can use our freedom to influence how we think, feel and act.

**"Wouldn't it be wonderful if we could all be more mindful of our freedom?"**

Here's an example: sometimes when I'm cycling I get stressed out by the boorish behaviour of some car drivers. Mindfulness enables me to freely influence my thought patterns and react more calmly to provocations on the road. I tell myself: 'these drivers are probably more stressed than me; I'm the lucky one, enjoying a nice cycle ride.' Instead of sticking up two fingers at angry drivers, I often smile at them.

Meditating on our freedom reminds us that mindful acceptance is *engaged acceptance*. In mindfulness we accept our experiences calmly and detachedly, not because we want to live passively, but – quite the opposite – because accepting our experiences creates for us a space in which we can freely engage with our lives. There are countless ways in which we can shape our lives mindfully; we can consciously decide whether we ought to endorse our thoughts (as true, useful or good) or reject them (as false, unhelpful or bad); we can reflect on whether or not our emotions are justified or excessive or harmful; we can deliberately downplay some inner forces and play up others, thus shaping our actions according to an overall plan of our own choosing.

Psychologists talk about the brain's 'executive functions'. Roughly speaking, these are the functions by which the brain consciously monitors and directs its activity. They include such abilities as controlling attention, inhibiting emotions and feelings, thinking flexibly, solving problems, reasoning, and planning. Taken together, these abilities sound a lot like mindfulness. Indeed, research suggests that meditation can strengthen our executive functions, thus giving us greater control over our lives.

But we must be careful here not to fall back into the one-sided trap of materialism. It is true that mindfulness must be produced by a mechanism in the brain, and must affect this mechanism, otherwise mindfulness wouldn't be part of our lives. But mindfulness is also *more* than a mechanism, because the self and freedom are more than a mechanism. The only way to make sense of this dichotomy is through a two-sided theory of human existence. The brain's executive functions are the basis of mindfulness but they do not fully account for mindfulness, because the brain's worldside cannot fully account for its selfside.

Mindfulness is a product of our executive functions – and vice versa. When we strengthen our executive functions through meditating we are, in effect, using mindfulness to make us more mindful in the future. Just as people tone up their muscles through using their muscles, we can tone up our mindfulness through being mindful.

And here's the most amazing thing: exercising our freedom, similarly, makes us more free. The more we consciously choose how to behave, the more we enhance our brain's executive functions, and the more we get into the habit of consciously choosing how to behave.

It sounds strange to think that freedom can become a habit. It sounds even stranger to say that we can get into the habit of choosing to be free. But that's how it goes when your brain is two-sided. From one perspective, your freedom is a habit, a mechanical tendency towards behaving freely. From another perspective, you *choose* to be free. Your self *makes itself* prominent; after all, your self is in control of itself – or, rather, you are in control of you. The more you choose freedom, the freer you'll be in future.

Of course, this invites another question: *should we act freely all the time?* In other words, should we always be self-awarely aware of what we are doing? Should we keep our selves prominent permanently, to keep a distance between our selves and our experiences, so that our actions and reactions can always be freely chosen?

At first sight, this sounds like a noble ideal. Wouldn't it be wonderful if we could live self-awarely and freely all the time? We'd never act impulsively or wantonly; we'd always act with deliberation and purpose.

Unfortunately, self-awareness has its downsides. For instance, it can make us somewhat indecisive. When we are constantly aware of our ability to choose, we risk being overwhelmed by an accumulation of options; paradoxically, too many choices can make it hard to choose, especially if some of the options that present themselves to us are equally attractive (or unattractive). We might even end up like Buridan's Ass, the hungry donkey who stood between two equidistant, equal-sized bales of hay, and couldn't decide which to approach first: he starved to death.

Self-awareness can also make us feel phoney. If we always make our choices in self-awareness – that is, if we always exercise self-control – we may come to feel as though we're acting out a part, forcing ourselves to say and do things that, deep down, we don't really want to. We all feel phoney sometimes. Who amongst us hasn't, say, laughed loudly through gritted teeth at an unfunny joke told by the boss? Or pretended to be pleased after receiving a dubious gift? Sometimes acts of self-control can be admirably polite. Other times they can be cowardly – for instance, when we hide in self-consciousness instead of condemning people's bad behaviour. Either way, most of us feel that the idea of being constantly self-aware is somewhat repugnant; we don't want to have to be on duty permanently, like a lifeguard, or an exam invigilator, or a master of ceremonies.

Relatedly, an excess of self-awareness can also make us feel unconfident. When we undertake too many of our actions self-consciously we may soon find that we lack conviction; we may even feel apathetic about the choices we make. 'Self-consciousness | like arthritis, weakens the grip', as the poet Rebecca Watts puts it.

In turn, self-awareness can lead us into wishful thinking, in which our lack of confidence warps into overconfidence. When we're feeling unsure, we sometimes overcompensate by mustering up a delusional faith in the force of our willpower; to gee ourselves up we kid ourselves about what we can achieve. As a result, we lose touch with reality, whether the reality of the situation we're in, or of our abilities and propensities.

The philosopher Alan Watts has nicely summed up what is wrong with excessive self-awareness: total self-control is a contradiction. If we controlled ourselves fully, we'd thwart ourselves fully. To avoid that fate, we need to retain our capacity for naturalness and spontaneity.

So now we have a new question: *should we always be spontaneous?* In the US and Europe during the 1960s the popular answer to this question was: yes. The so-called 'Swinging Sixties' saw the emergence of a youth counterculture that railed against the stuffy self-control of the older generation. Hippies and mods and rockers and folkies all encouraged each other to express themselves, do whatever 'felt good', let it all hang out, and lose their inhibitions (often under the influence of drugs).

It started out as a bit of fun. Alas, it didn't last. Total spontaneity gives license to negative impulses as well as positive ones. Anyone who has ever scrutinised their inner experience will know that not every idea or impulse that flits through the mind ought to be vented in action. All sorts of scary and grotesque creatures lurk in the depths of human consciousness. Unconstrained, these monsters emerged from the darkness and made a mockery of the 'peace and love' ethos of the 1960s; the dream became a nightmare. 'Free love' communes fell apart in acrimony and jealousy. Music festivals descended into mayhem and fighting. In the general population, violent crime rose precipitately (and didn't abate until three decades later). Crazily, intellectuals and artists of the day often glorified crime by portraying criminals as rebellious heroes of spontaneity.

Taken to excess, spontaneity is a form of self-escape – a means of evading freedom and responsibility. Not uncoincidentally, the 1960s also saw a surge of interest in 'Transcendental Meditation' (inspired by Maharishi Mahesh Yogi, whose teachings were rooted in Hinduism) and Zen Buddhism. Both these schools of thought tended to promote meditation as a way to overcome the so-called illusion of being an individual self. Freedom became equated in many people's minds not with self-awareness but with being *free from oneself*. Meditation became the handmaiden of spontaneity.

It may sound controversial to link meditation to wantonness and violence. To be fair to Buddhism and Hinduism, both religions contain many, many condemnations of violence, as well as a huge amount of nuanced debate about the existence of the self. And even when meditation unequivocally is practised as a means to transcend the self, the actual outcome, ironically, can be an increase in self-awareness. The Buddhist text *Majjhima Nikaya* contains the following description of a self-less person: 'In walking, standing, sitting or lying down he understands that he is so doing, so that, however his body is engaged, he understands it just as it is … In setting out or returning, or in looking before or around, in bending or stretching his arm … he acts with clear awareness.' This sounds more like a recipe for always acting with self-awareness than for never doing so.

Yet anyone interested in mindfulness ought to be honest about the fact that in the Eastern tradition there are explicit connections between violence and the doctrine of no-self. Here is an alarming extract from the Buddhist text *Jueguan Iun*: 'The fire in the bush burns the mountain; the hurricane breaks trees; the collapsing cliff crushes wild animals to death; the running mountain's stream drowns the insects. If a man can make his mind similar [to these forces], then, meeting a man, he may kill him all the same.' In a similar passage, the Zen Master Takuan noted that when a man strikes another man with a sword, neither of them 'are possessed of a mind that has any substantiality'.

In Hinduism an entire holy book, the *Bhagavad Gita*, is dedicated to the practice of waging war. Once again we find that killers are exonerated, and victims dehumanised, by the idea that there is no such thing as an individual self. Every individual is supposedly absorbed into a universal consciousness that 'neither kills, nor is it killed'.

Historically, Buddhism and Hinduism have been used, like any religion, to justify violence. Notoriously, during the Second World War, the Japanese military used Zen teachings to inspire its soldiers, with the support of many Zen leaders. The doctrine of no-self motivated extreme personal sacrifices, including those of kamikaze suicide pilots. When you don't have a self, you cannot suffer or die; in war, duty becomes your only goal. The Nazis were particularly impressed by the motivational power of Zen. Hitler himself exclaimed: 'Why didn't we have the religion of the Japanese, who regard sacrifice for the Fatherland as the highest good?'

Needless to say, not all self-escapers display wanton behaviour or violent tendencies. But it is disconcerting to find that many of today's proponents of mindfulness are still blithely championing the doctrine of no-self. The writer Michael Taft gives us the following advice: 'Simply notice no-self. As you sink into the experience more deeply and fully over time, no-self will become a tremendously empowering, enlivening, and enlightening (no)thing. If you see that there is no-self, you'll see that there is no one to have any problems. And that is something worth noticing.'

Perhaps we should let history be the judge of that.

Few people today go as far as glorifying criminals, but materialism has become the prevailing philosophy of modern intellectuals, and materialism, like the doctrine of no-self, exonerates bad behaviour. If being a material brain is all there is to being human, then none of us are truly responsible for what we do. If we cannot freely influence our behaviour, then we are always beholden to the inner and outer forces that impose themselves upon us (including such forces as our emotions, our genetic influences, our upbringing and our social circumstances). The former prison psychiatrist Theodore Dalrymple has noted that criminals often have a strangely passive attitude to their wrongdoing. They say things such as 'the knife went in', or 'the gun went off'; they refuse to accept any personal responsibility. Even more strangely, intellectuals who are influenced by materialism often support the self-exculpatory fantasies of wrongdoers.

Of course, it is true that sometimes there are gross neurological abnormalities that explain bad behaviour. But most wrongdoers know precisely what they're doing: they're indulging themselves at someone else's expense. And they know that the very reason they seek exoneration is that they don't want their future choices to be circumscribed by punishment or by feelings of conscience. In most cases, denying the existence of the self is both false and harmful, to the wrongdoers and to their victims. Both are 'possessed of a mind that has any substantiality' – that's what makes crime crime.

No, we cannot escape from the downsides of constant self-awareness by trying to convince ourselves that total spontaneity is virtuous or inevitable. Somehow we must find a suitable balance between self-awareness and spontaneity. And we must try to ensure that our spontaneity remains true to the non-impulsive decisions we make in self-awareness.

Thankfully, mindfulness can help us to achieve both these outcomes. In meditation, we discover that mindfulness and spontaneity are not opposed to each other – far from it. Being mindful often leads us into a mental state that psychologists call being in 'flow'. Flow is when a situation or task absorbs our attention to such a degree that we are aware of nothing but what we are doing; our self-awareness recedes behind the prominence of our practical awareness. I'm sure you can think of an activity that puts you in flow – knitting, dancing, woodwork, fixing cars, playing a musical instrument, playing sports, or whatever. When we perform activities such as these, we typically begin self-consciously and deliberately, but soon become totally engrossed.

Mindfulness leads us into flow, because, in self-aware awareness, our acceptance of our thoughts, sensations and feelings enables us to disentangle ourselves from them, whereupon our anxiety decreases and our focus shifts to the outside world; we get on with living. And, of course, the whole point of mindfulness is to cultivate an attitude of engaged acceptance, whereby we reflect on our experiences so as to act upon those reflections. When we live like this, our actions are spontaneous in the sense that we don't always need to exercise self-control to carry out those actions effectively – indeed, self-control is a hindrance to most actions – yet, because of their origins in mindfulness, our actions remain an expression of our self-awareness and freedom.

Even the most incorrigibly spontaneous people remain free throughout their spontaneity. This is because even a recessive self is free to be prominent. No matter how wantonly we behave, no matter how much disregard we show for our responsibility, we cannot escape the fact that we remain free to act freely: the self doesn't disappear when it is recessive any more than reality disappears amid uncertainty. The problem with people who fetishise spontaneity is that they kid themselves about their capacity for self-control so as to indulge themselves wantonly. In contrast, when we execute spontaneous actions in mindfulness, we imbue those actions with an implicit reminder of our freedom, a reminder that we can return to freedom at any point to revise or refine our choices. It is as if mindfulness ushers our actions into the world with a memory bracelet attached to them, to remind us to return to freedom whenever the resolutions we made in freedom are in jeopardy. Consider again the example of me cycling mindfully: I begin my ride mindfully, then I glide into flow, but I imbue my sense of flow with a reminder that, if I find myself getting aggravated by boorish drivers, I must return to self-awareness.

The state of being tacitly aware of our freedom even when we are acting spontaneously could be called *remindfulness*. This state is an important part of mindfulness. Remindfulness is how mindfulness echoes in spontaneous behaviour, enabling us to return us to our freedom whenever we hit obstacles. Moreover, remindfulness is how we naturally return to mindfulness even when things are going well. Like a boomerang arcing back to its owner, we return remindfully to mindfulness to await further instructions on how to act.

This oscillation between mindfulness and remindfulness answers the question of how freely and how spontaneously we should act. Or rather, the actual experience of being mindful answers the question for each of us as individuals. When we resolve to live mindfully, mindfulness tells us when to flow and when to be self-aware, when to choose, when to be spontaneous, and when to choose again. By obeying the voice of mindfulness, we decline to stay relentlessly self-aware. Conversely, remindfulness prevents us from flowing impulsively and wantonly. Flow becomes mindful flow; that is, spontaneity becomes mindful spontaneity.

I think this conclusion is an apt response to the problem of existential anxiety. When we try to escape ourselves and renounce our freedom, we do so because we believe that *being free here now* is intolerable. Whether we fear losing control, or whether we fear our responsibilities, we feel that the burden of existing is simply too much to bear; better to be no one at all than an overburdened self. In putting us calmly back in touch with ourselves *and* reality, mindfulness puts our freedom to work again, *for* us, not *against* us – not as a menace to our equanimity but as a friend to our plans and prospects.

Like any good friend, mindfulness persuades us to be realistic about the scope of our freedom. In mindfulness, we learn about the inner and outer forces that shape our experience. We learn about unfreedom, not because we want to make better excuses for ourselves, but because we want to become more free. We learn to harness and ride the forces of the world and of our minds, and we learn to drive some inner demons back down into the depths where they belong.

Above all, perhaps, mindfulness enables us to sculpt our own spontaneous habits. The more we execute actions deliberately in mindfulness, the more spontaneous those actions become. We fake it till we make it, like a musician who consciously and deliberately learns a performance, so that he can perform with spontaneous excellence.

We can never master the relentless forces of imposition that shape our experience, but in mindful freedom we may just be able to prevent ourselves from being mastered by them.

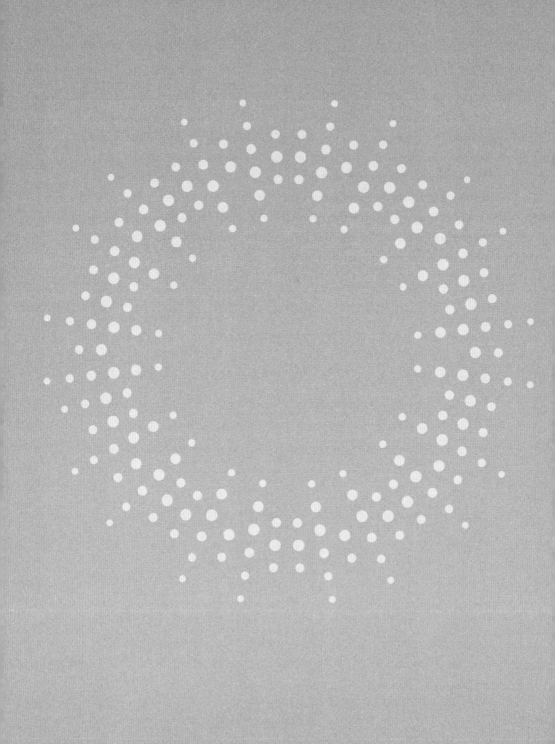

# Five

## Is There a Higher Power?

There is a story about a philosophy professor who set his students a tricky exam question. The question contained a single word: Why? Apparently, one student received top marks for the simplest of answers: Because. Hearing this, you may be tempted to roll your eyes. But, actually, this exchange contains a wealth of profundity. The exam question hints at two perennial mysteries. First, the mystery of whether or not our universe has a hidden source – whether or not there is a higher power. Second, the mystery of why anything at all exists – why there isn't nothing. Some say that we can only solve the second mystery by solving the first. And some just say ... Because. The student who received the top marks was onto something – something hidden in plain sight.

**I**magine, if you will, that you are lying on your back in a dimly lit room, staring up at a blank wall, when suddenly you are paralysed with fear. A bewildering image has appeared on the wall, shimmering into existence like an apparition. The image, which covers the entire wall, looks like an aerial shot of a maze. As you stare upwards, wide-eyed, unable to move a muscle, a little blue dot suddenly appears and begins to scurry through the maze's channels. It seems, to your strange fancy, that the blue dot is running away, trying to reach sanctuary at the edge of the maze. For the blue dot is not alone.

A red dot has appeared too, and is faster and more determined than the blue dot. The red dot catches the blue dot and obliterates it. But no sooner has the blue dot disappeared than another one pops up elsewhere in the maze. This blue newcomer, like its predecessor, begins to scurry towards safety but, once again, is chased down and obliterated by the red dot. Again and again, it happens. Blue dot, red dot, killed. Blue dot, red dot, killed. As you watch, with no choice but to witness this grim spectacle, your fear turns to dismay, then to revulsion, then to terror. Yet, at the same time, you sense that what you are witnessing is somehow profound, indeed revelatory. The problem is, you don't know what exactly is being revealed to you. Perhaps you are afraid because you are blind to the secret; or perhaps you are blind to the secret because you are afraid.

I have just described to you a vivid hallucination I experienced when, aged ten, I was feverish with the flu. In the ensuing years, I became obsessed with finding out what, if anything, was revealed to me that day. In my early adulthood, when my existential anxiety began in earnest and I took refuge in philosophy, I continued to return in my mind to that hallucination.

I know it sounds dippy, but I was convinced that the maze and the dots were, in some obscure way, symbolic of life itself. After all, I was no less bewildered by the hallucination than by my own existence.

Indeed, it seemed to me that the hallucination and my existence had much in common. I was like the blue dot, I reckoned, and reality was like the red dot; reality was always there, relentlessly assailing me, and ultimately it would catch up with me and annihilate me. I wanted to escape from being here now. Perhaps, beyond the edge of reality, there existed a higher power, a power that could defy the forces of death; perhaps there was such a thing as salvation. If I could get there, whether during my lifetime or after it, I might experience the profoundest of revelations. Through understanding how the higher power could cheat death, I would understand why anything, rather than nothing, exists; I would understand why the universe is here.

I wasn't the first, and I won't be the last, to seek salvation from – and, thereby, an explanation for – existence. Who amongst us has never hoped, whether quietly or fervently, that the universe has an inspirational hidden source? Since time immemorial humanity has sought consolation and edification in a higher power. Some call it God; others call it the Supreme Being, the Absolute, the Creator, the Almighty, the Tao, the Universal Consciousness, Nirvana, Enlightenment, Liberation, or Oneness. Some simply call it Love.

Whatever you call it, people are desperate to reach it; like refugees, their eyes are fixed on a promised land. An *existential refugee*, shall we say, is someone who seeks to escape from human existence altogether by escaping from his self *and* from the world. In seeking a higher power, the aim is to find inspiration, yet the trigger for the search is existential anxiety. The notion of a higher power is not as life-affirming as it sounds.

This chapter is about whether salvation is possible or truly desirable. It is about whether we can make sense of the idea of escaping to a place where we will discover that the existence we escaped from never really existed. It is about whether we can genuinely find inspiration by reaching a place where we don't need inspiration anymore. It is about whether existence can really be explained by a higher power, or whether, rather, a higher power is itself inexplicable. It is about whether the world, on its own, is sufficient to explain why the world exists. It is about what my strange hallucination really meant.

Above all, it is about what is revealed to us when we stop looking for revelations, and instead pay mindful attention to being here now. In the end, I gave up searching for a higher power. And that was when I found what I was looking for.

## The Godside

God is the most popular destination for existential refugees. How come? Where do they think they're going? What is God? It's tempting to quote Louis Armstrong again: 'If you've gotta ask, you ain't never gonna get to know.' After all, if salvation is possible, then God exists beyond our minds and beyond reality – so we're never gonna get to know him until we reach him, by which time we won't need to ask callow questions about him anymore. Many believers admit that we can't even know for sure that God exists. We must show faith, they say. Religious faith is a synonym for 'there can be no conclusive proof of God's existence, but I believe in him anyway'.

Despite making this admission, many believers also claim to be able to understand what God is like. If God exists, they say, then there are some characteristics he possesses by definition. These characteristics are defined in opposition to the universe beyond which God purportedly exists.

Everything in our universe is limited in power, size, knowledge, goodness and duration; therefore, so it goes, if God exists beyond this mortal coil, he is limitless in each of those respects; he is omnipotent, infinite, omniscient, perfectly good and eternal.

Most believers also conclude that God is conscious. Everything that exists in the worldside of human existence is *unconscious* (that's why the selfside of our existence must be unworldly). Therefore, if God exists, he is an unworldly, limitless consciousness existing beyond our own consciousness. In this way, God supposedly fills our lives with purpose and promise; our true purpose is his purpose, and the promise of our lives is his promise that we can be saved. To some extent, we can be saved in the here and now, by being protected and inspired by God, but, above all, we can be saved at the end of our lives – saved, perhaps, from something worse than life.

The idea that we can be saved by God implies that, at present, we are as independent from God as he is from us; if we were already under God's full control, we wouldn't need to be saved. Hence, even though human existence was created by God's higher power, the powers of the self and reality operate independently of his power, like a probe sent by scientists to a far-off planet. Our existence derives from God, but, aside from performing the occasional miracle, he is not the last word on being here now. We are *of* him, but not entirely *in* him.

There is much debate among believers in God about what exactly the self and reality are. There are believers who are idealists, dualists and even materialists. However, having debunked these doctrines in previous chapters, let's try to understand God (and the various other higher powers) in relation to the only theory still standing, namely, a two-sided theory according to which the self and the brain are opposites unified. God, on this view, is a third side to human existence; our existence contains a selfside, a worldside, and … let's call it a Godside. In a two-sided theory, the selfside derives its existence from the worldside (i.e. consciousness arises from the brain), but is independent of the worldside. In a three-sided theory, the selfside and the worldside both derive their existence from a Godside, but are independent of the Godside.

A three-sided theory sounds neat and tidy. However, when we start really probing the idea of a Godside, the whole notion collapses like a house of cards.

By definition, a Godside would be *neither* the selfside nor the worldside of human existence, yet, at the same time, the Godside would include *both* the selfside and the worldside, because both derive their existence from the Godside. This definition is rather baroque but it fits our intuitive understanding of what God is; he is supposed to exist beyond human existence (he is *neither* the self nor the world), and his higher power is supposed to be the basis of our existence (he is *both* the self and the world).

The problem is, the area between the selfside and the worldside is crowded, and there's no room for a Godside. Take a look, once again, at the model of human existence we made in chapter two. Notice how human existence is *already* neither a selfside nor a worldside. The self opposes the world; the world recedes when the self is prominent. And the world opposes the self; the self recedes when the world is prominent. In other words, the self and the world negate each other. So, insofar as our existence contains both a selfside and a worldside, our existence already contains neither.

But, hang on – surely if our existence already contains neither a self nor a world then there *is* a Godside? It's not that simple. When we say that our existence already contains neither a self nor a world, we are not adding anything to the idea that the self and the world exist. The negation of the self arises from the existence of the world; and the negation of the world arises from the existence of the self. Neither is both – and that's all there is to it. Together, the self and the world are neither and both – neither being both, and both being neither.

On this reckoning, the Godside is either underwhelming or overwhelming. If God is supposed to be neither the self nor the world *but both at the same time*, then he is underwhelming; he adds nothing to human existence. Our existence is already both the self and the world and neither. God can hardly offer us salvation if he adds nothing to the situation he's supposed to save us from.

Alternatively, if God is supposed to be neither the self nor the world *but without also being both*, then he is overwhelming; he engulfs the self and the world, and, in so doing, destroys the independence of human existence. After all, God is supposed to be the basis of everything that exists. If the self and the world belong to a God that is neither of them without being both, then the self and the world, by definition, would not exist *as a self and a world*. They'd be utterly different from what we thought they were. Like a face in a cloud, a face that turned out to be nothing but cloud, the self and the world would turn out to be nothing but God. And, once again, salvation would become meaningless; if human existence is indistinguishable from God, we're never apart from him.

The underwhelming-overwhelming dilemma shows up, subtly, in some other arguments against God. Atheists often argue that God couldn't have created human freedom, because if he were omniscient and omnipotent he'd know and control all the choices we make, in which case we wouldn't really be free. In other words, an omniscient and omnipotent God would be overwhelming; he'd engulf our freedom. Alternatively, perhaps God isn't omniscient and omnipotent; perhaps he lives on this mortal coil of ours; perhaps he created freedom out of the ingredients of the world. But in that case, God would be underwhelming. We already know that the world creates freedom via the brain; God adds nothing to that explanation.

The underwhelming-overwhelming dilemma also shows up in the idea that a perfectly good God created suffering. Atheists often argue that God cannot be the source of our lives, because if he were omnipotent and perfectly good then he'd be powerful enough and good enough to spare us from suffering. To defend God's power and goodness, theists often argue that there must be something good about suffering. Even an event as terrible as the detonation in 1945 of a nuclear bomb over Hiroshima, British philosopher Richard Swinburne once suggested, created an 'opportunity' for 'courage and sympathy'. Eurgh! Clearly, a God that twists all human suffering into goodness is grotesquely overwhelming; he converts our pain into his own so-called moral perfection. Alternatively, if God is neither perfectly good nor omnipotent – if he is as corruptible and fallible as anything else in our world – then he is underwhelming; he cannot add anything to our understanding of suffering. Imperfection begets imperfection; we already know this.

I think the idea that a perfectly good God created an imperfect universe is deeply troubling. Believers seem to think that God will save them from the very same situation to which God subjected them in the first place. Whenever I hear believers say that God created the world so that he could lovingly save us from it, I can't help thinking of the psychiatric condition known as Stockholm syndrome, in which people who are held captive grow to love their captor. Sometimes captives are so imperilled by their captivity, they feel that they will be safer if they enter into extreme sympathy with their captor than if they resist him. Believers in God, in a similar fashion, seem to have fallen in love with God, their existential captor.

That's why ardent believers rarely respond rationally when doubters point out the discrepancy between God's so-called love for us and his decision to entrap us in a world that contains suffering. To an ardent believer, any reason to fear God is another reason to blindly love God.

Mercifully, it is pointless to fall in love with God or to try to escape from him. If we are here now – and we most certainly are – then the Godside is underwhelming or overwhelming. Either way, salvation is impossible. If God is underwhelming, he can't save us, because he adds nothing to the existence we're already in. If he's overwhelming, he can't save us, because there'd be no such thing as a human existence to save us from.

## Beardless Gods

Sophisticated existential refugees warn against attributing human-like qualities to a higher power. A higher power, they say, is not like the proverbial 'bearded man in the sky' who judges us, punishes us, loves us and responds to our prayers; if we insist that such a figure exists, and if we insist on trying to understand his motives rather than slavishly worshipping him, we will inevitably become confused and disillusioned; we may even become resentful, like the character Riddick who declares in the film *Pitch Black*, 'I absolutely believe in God. And I absolutely hate the fucker'.

The idea of a higher power comes in a range of versions, most of which can be found in Eastern as well as Western traditions. At one end of the spectrum are higher powers that are construed as very human-like. At the other end are higher powers that are construed as very abstract. In all these various versions, the higher power is construed as the source of the self and the world; in other words, according to a two-sided theory of human existence, each higher power is a third side in which the selfside and the worldside originate.

The oldest and most influential Eastern religion is Hinduism. Hindus believe in a higher power called 'Brahman'. Like any higher power, Brahman exists beyond the world and beyond the individual self (which Hindus call 'atman'). In existing beyond the world, Brahman is conscious, but, having created everything, Brahman is everywhere: a universal consciousness. In turn, each atman, like a drop in the ocean, is part of the universal consciousness. Brahman is a cosmic oneness from which no person or thing is differentiable.

This outline makes Brahman sound very much like God. However, in Hindu theology Brahman is usually described as an impersonal power — as, say, an ultimate reality or creative principle, as opposed to a bearded overlord. Hindus believe that we can reach salvation only by accepting that everything originates in Brahman. The stakes are even higher for Hindu existential refugees than for believers in God. According to Hinduism, when we die we are 'reincarnated', that is, we are reborn into the body of another person or animal. Whether we are reborn into hardship or happiness will depend, so it goes, on how well we behave during our lifetime. Good people are reborn into good fortune; bad people into misfortune. We get our just desserts in future lives; this is known as the doctrine of 'karma'. The only way we can escape from repeatedly being reincarnated is to acknowledge that in Brahman we exist beyond the circle of life and death. When we acknowledge this, Hindus say, we achieve 'moksha', a blissful state of 'liberation'; we ensure that this life will be our last.

For all its beguiling poetry, the idea of reincarnation doesn't make sense if the human self is an aspect of the human brain. If you are the selfside of your brain, you will no longer exist when your brain ceases to exist. You cannot be reborn as another human being or animal if you cannot exist without your own brain.

Nor does the idea of Brahman make sense if you are the selfside of your brain. Like God, Brahman is either underwhelming or overwhelming.

Brahman is underwhelming if its power adds nothing to human existence. At first sight, this outcome seems unlikely, because Brahman is defined as existing beyond the self and beyond the world. However, in order to draw our attention to Brahman, Hindus argue that neither the self nor the world truly exists. And sometimes, it seems, this strategy backfires: Hindus end up arguing against the self and the world by arguing *for*, respectively, the world and the self.

For instance, in chapter three we saw that Hindus claim that the world is 'maya' – an illusion. An illusion arguably requires an experiencer, so, in effect, Hindus seem to deny the existence of the world by invoking the existence of the self. In turn, we saw in chapter four that Hindus also claim that the individual self is an illusion. They often express this idea by declaring 'that art thou' while gesturing around them, indicating, one might assume, that there is no difference between *thou* (your self) and *that* (everything else in the world). In effect, Hindus seem to deny the existence of the self by invoking the existence of the world.

On this reckoning, Brahman is neither the self nor the world, but only insofar as the self and the world both exist. A so-called higher power of this kind would be underwhelming, incapable of providing salvation.

Perhaps this definition doesn't do justice to Brahman. After all, Hindus define Brahman not only negatively (i.e. as neither the self nor the world) but positively, as a universal consciousness. On this view, when Hindus declare 'that are thou', what they really mean is 'a universal consciousness art thou'. And when they describe the world as maya, what they really mean is that the world is an illusion experienced by an illusory self, because only the universal consciousness is real. But this definition doesn't make the idea of Brahman any more plausible. If Brahman is defined as neither the self nor the world, and not both, then Brahman is overwhelming. Like a face in a cloud – nothing but cloud – human existence would be engulfed by Brahman, in which case there would be nowhere for us to be saved from.

You don't have to be religious to believe in salvation. Plenty of philosophers who are atheists believe that the universe is governed by a higher power. Most of these philosophers would baulk at the idea that they are seeking salvation, but I think the word is apt. All people, whether theists or atheists, who seek a higher power do so because they are existential refugees; they are consoled by the idea that human existence is something other than what it seems to be, that it emanates from someplace else.

Some atheist philosophers, like theists, believe that the source of all things is conscious. However, these philosophers do not believe in a single, unified, omnipresent consciousness, such as God or Brahman. Rather, they believe in a plural, diverse, omnipresent consciousness. According to this idea, known as 'panpsychism', everything is comprised of lots of little bits of consciousness – 'mind dust', as William James evocatively put it.

Panpsychists disagree amongst themselves about what exactly mind dust is and how it works. Numerous possibilities suggest themselves. Maybe there are atoms or elements of consciousness, and these combine to form the contents of our universe. Maybe the fundamental particles identified by physicists are conscious. Maybe every object, no matter how big or small, is conscious. Maybe consciousness stacks up inside itself like Russian dolls, so that if a car is conscious, then its engine is also conscious, and the parts of its engine are conscious, and so on.

All these forms of panpsychism have a common – now familiar – defect: they're overwhelming or underwhelming. Look around at the world. If the objects you perceive are, deep down, not really real, if each object is nothing more than a welter of minds, if the universe is consciousness through and through, then consciousness would overwhelm the reality of everything. Dr Johnson would be perfectly entitled to refute this barmy idea with his boot.

Similarly, mind dust, if it existed, would destroy the integrity of your self. Each time you made a choice, your choice would not really be your own. It would be the choice of a committee, indeed a rabble – the rabble of all the tiny minds that comprise your consciousness. Mind dust would overwhelm your freedom.

Panpsychists respond to these objections by insisting that mind dust can create real objects and individual human selves. Perhaps when the right type and the right amount of mind dust comes together in the right way, real objects can suddenly crystallise into existence. And perhaps when lots of minds come together in the right way they can congeal into a single decision-maker, like a football team that plays as a single unit through having a good team spirit. In other words, although mind dust is *neither* a (human) self nor a world (because mind dust isn't a single self, and isn't reality), perhaps mind dust can also be *both* the self and the world. The problem, of course, is that the self and the world are *already* neither a self nor a world. Unless mind dust is neither the self nor the world *without being both*, it is underwhelming.

By now you may be beginning to suspect that any attempt to identify a higher power will be thwarted by the underwhelming-overwhelming dilemma. And you'd be right! But, in each case, the reasons why are subtle.

According to one influential idea in philosophy, the higher power that governs our universe is *mathematics*. On the face of it, this idea is more plausible than a conscious higher power. After all, as Galileo remarked, the book of nature is written in the language of mathematics.

But Galileo didn't say the book of nature is *made out of* mathematics. Mathematics arguably has too much power for that. Most philosophers believe that mathematical truths are necessary. Necessary truths must be true; they cannot not be true. For instance, $2 + 2 = 4$ cannot not be true. Pythagoras's theorem, which declares that the square of the hypotenuse of a right-angled triangle is equal to the sum of the squares of the triangle's other two sides, cannot not be true. The statement that there are infinitely many prime numbers cannot not be true. And so on. Maths, so it goes, is truth with a capital T.

In an attempt to make sense of mathematical necessity, some philosophers (and many mathematicians) argue that numbers and other mathematical entities, such as lines and curves and shapes, exist in an abstract realm of eternal and unchanging truths. This theory is often called 'Platonism', after the ancient Greek philosopher Plato who advocated it. Some thinkers, including Plato himself, go as far as to say that an abstract realm of mathematics is the source of the universe and everything in it, including the human self.

The problem with the idea of mathematics as a higher power is that, if true, it would make every aspect of human existence necessary – and this seems deeply implausible. After all, the truths that our universe contains *might not* have been true. To see this, pick any truth you like, and then try to imagine circumstances in which that particular truth would not have been true. For instance, consider the truth that the Allies won the Second World War. They might not have won it; Hitler might not have overstretched his forces by invading Russia; the Americans might not have entered the war; and so on. Truth in our universe has a small t; no truth is necessarily true.

The same goes – even more obviously – for the contents of your self. The choices you make in life are not necessary, nor are the beliefs you hold;

you might have chosen otherwise or held different beliefs. If mathematical truths were a higher power they'd engulf human existence with their necessity – they'd be overwhelming.

Some philosophers are so wary of Platonism, they are willing to downgrade mathematical truths to a more mundane status. Perhaps mathematics doesn't involve necessary truths at all. Perhaps mathematical truths are mere hypotheses that can be revised depending on our experience; for instance, we might one day discover that $2 + 2 = 5$. Perhaps human beings invented the rules of mathematics in the same way that we invent the rules of games. Perhaps the rules of mathematics stem from the way our brains are designed.

Or perhaps mathematical truths are in one sense necessary and in another sense non-necessary. According to this view, mathematical truths are laws that are necessarily true within our universe, but these laws *might not* have been true, because our universe might have had different necessary laws. This kind of watered-down necessity could be called *quasi-necessity*; the big T of quasi-necessary truth is just a special kind of small t. Mathematical truths, so it goes, do indeed have a special status; they do indeed exist 'beyond' the self and reality, but only insofar as our universe exists.

Perhaps. The point is, if mathematical truths are mundane in any of these various ways, then mathematics would be unable to explain where human existence came from. Hypotheses, made-up rules, quirks of human psychology and quasi-necessary truths would be underwhelming as higher powers.

Even mathematics fails as a higher power. Should we throw up our hands in exasperation? Or, indeed, in exultation? Some people say that we can only solve the mystery of our origins when we embrace the mystery for what it is.

## Demystifying Mystery

As strange as it sounds, plenty of philosophers and religious believers argue that the key to understanding our existence is to accept that we cannot understand our existence. The problem, they say, is that we keep trying to *describe* the higher power that created our universe, but the higher power is, by nature, indescribable. After all, descriptions belong to human existence; a description involves a *self* describing *reality*. Only by giving up on descriptions, so it goes, can we identify the higher power that exists beyond ourselves and reality.

> "Mystics claim to possess intuitive knowledge of an unworldly higher power"

This intriguing view is known as 'mysticism', the idea being that the higher power that created our universe is, and must remain, a total mystery. In the West, mysticism is usually associated with New Age types who believe in UFOs and the healing power of crystals. But, in fact, one of the most technical, hard-nosed and ingenious Western philosophers of all time was, to all intents and purposes, a mystic: Immanuel Kant.

Kant believed that the self and the world stem from a 'noumenal' realm that exists forever beyond human description. Although we can know that this noumenal realm exists, insisted Kant, we can never know of its content; it must remain a mere '$x$' in our understanding. Despite this downbeat verdict, Kant wrote extensively about the unknowability of the noumenal realm. It is tempting to wonder why he bothered. Some philosophers argue that Kant's work was worthwhile, because he provided us with knowledge about the limits of our knowledge. Other philosophers argue that his conclusions were meaningless, because if the noumenal realm is unknowable and indescribable, then how can we know it is there, and how can we refer to it at all?

Kant believed in the existence of a noumenal realm because, in his words, he 'had to deny knowledge in order to make room for faith'. In other words, Kant saw mysticism as a way of creating a space for God. But not all mystics – especially religious mystics – agree that we can never know anything about the proposed mysterious higher power. These optimistic mystics claim to have plenty of mystical knowledge, but there's a catch: they can't communicate what they know.

How can they know if they can't say? The clue is in the question: optimistic mystics claim to have *intuitive* knowledge – knowledge that cannot be captured in thoughts and words. This idea is not as lame as it sounds. Often in life we have knowledge of things we can't adequately describe. Think of someone you love; can you fully describe their face? Can you fully describe your exact emotional state at this very moment? Inadequate descriptions leave something out: the indescribable.

Of course, these examples of indescribability come from our world. In contrast, mystics claim to possess intuitive knowledge of an unworldly higher power. All the major religions include mystical sects that, supposedly, show us how to acquire this intuitive knowledge. Judaism and Islam include the sects of Kabbalah and Sufism, respectively, while Christianity incorporated mystical ideas as far back as the second century AD. Mystic believers claim that we can gain intuitive knowledge of God through prayer, contemplation, ecstatic worship and various other meditative practices.

Hindus believe, similarly, that we can come to know Brahman intuitively through the practice of meditation. Through focusing on the idea of Brahman, a meditator can supposedly move his awareness beyond himself and the world; in doing so, he allows himself to be completely absorbed in Brahman, so that the self and its world are unmasked as illusions, and Brahman's oneness becomes apparent.

Religious mystics declare that when we know a higher power through intuition the experience is a blissful one. But even mystical knowledge can make its knower resentful. Anyone who claims to be acquainted with a higher power also knows, deep down, that that higher power is responsible for creating suffering. Occasionally a mystic comes along who not only refuses to be captor-bonded, but is actively hostile to the higher power he experiences. One such rebel was Arthur Schopenhauer.

In one of the most original and evocative moves in the history of Western philosophy, Schopenhauer argued that we can gain intuitive knowledge of a mystical realm via the nature of our own willpower. Schopenhauer, you will recall, believed that all objects contain a hidden essence, a blind striving, surging, willing. We gain intuitive insight into this hidden essence, he insisted, whenever we wilfully impose ourselves upon the world around us. Our conscious willpower, so it goes, has a sort of mystical underbelly; our willpower emanates from the same blind will that is contained in everything.

Far from making us feel blissful, this intuitive knowledge ought to appal us, Schopenhauer concluded. In a world where all is will, where the will 'feeds upon itself', where every thing 'exists at the expense of another', non-existence is preferable to the 'torment and agony' of existence. Mercifully, Schopenhauer claimed, human beings are uniquely able to turn against the source of our existence; we can will the cessation of our willing. In doing so, we can extinguish the will itself, leaving behind … nothing. This is salvation by way of a suicide-attack on a malevolent higher power.

Between Schopenhauer's implacable hostility and the bliss experienced by religious mystics, there is a more casual attitude one might take to the idea of a mystical higher power. This casual attitude tends to be found among mystic philosophers (Schopenhauer notwithstanding). It is also found in the ancient Chinese tradition of Taoism, which is somewhere between a religion and a philosophy. The Tao in Taoism means 'the Way': a spontaneous, creative principle that supposedly lies at the heart of all existence, and in which all things are unified. The Tao shouldn't be worshipped, but nor should it be resisted, say Taoists. Quite the contrary: human beings ought to strive to live in harmony with the Tao – to be spontaneous and creative, and cultivate an awareness that we are inseparable from the rest of nature. The Tao is a way to live, as well as the way things are.

It is hard to be more specific than this when talking about Taoism, because, after all, the Tao is a mystical realm that we can only know through intuition. As Lao Tzu, the founder of Taoism, famously explained: 'Those who know do not speak. Those who speak do not know.'

Another example of this casual attitude towards a mystical higher power can be seen in Platonism. Platonists believe that the way we gain access to the abstract realm of mathematical truths is through intuition. The thinking behind this idea is that mathematical truths have an element of indescribability; they can be seen, and baldly stated, but it is very hard to begin to say *why* they are true (why does $2 + 2 = 4$, for instance?). Though many mathematicians believe in mathematical intuition, few go as far as worshipping numbers. However, in ancient Greece there was a cult known as the Pythagoreans, whose members, following the cult's eponymous leader, Pythagoras, worshipped numbers and even made sacrifices to mathematical theorems!

By now, you are probably gaining the correct impression that, when it comes to describing (or indeed not describing) the idea of a higher power, there is some overlap between the various religions and philosophies. Moreover, within each religion or philosophy, there are many different strands and interpretations, and these also contribute to the overlap.

One thing that all the various higher powers have in common, of course, is that they all fall prey to the overwhelming-underwhelming dilemma, and mysticism is no exception. It's the same old story, whether the mysterious higher power is construed as a blissful state, a wilful inner essence, the Tao, a noumenal realm, an abstract mathematical realm, or whatever. In each case, the mystical realm is defined as neither the self nor the world. And, once again, the problem is that human existence *already* contains neither the self nor the world; being neither is no different from being a self in a world. If the mystical realm is neither the self nor the world, but also both, then a mysterious higher power adds nothing to human existence, and therefore is underwhelming. Alternatively, if the mystical realm is neither the self nor the world, *but not both*, then the mysterious higher power would overwhelm our existence: the self and the world would cease to exist; mystery would engulf both.

In either case, a mystical realm couldn't possibly provide salvation: we can't be saved by the situation we're already in, and we can't be saved if human existence doesn't really exist.

## From Riches to Rags to Nothing

There is one last hope for a higher power. I've kept this suggestion until last, because, although it displays familiar failings, it also points us towards a truly game-changing idea.

Fittingly, this last idea for a higher power came from an Indian prince who, around 2500 years ago, abandoned his former life of power and privilege, choosing instead to live amongst the poor. His name was Siddhartha Gautama, but he is better known as 'the Buddha'. According to legend, the Buddha's childhood was so sheltered that he was unaware that suffering existed, until the first day he ever left his palace home. He was so shocked by what he saw in the surrounding villages – sickness, poverty, death – he immediately renounced his wealth, and decided to devote his life to discovering the key to salvation.

On the face of it, the discoveries he made – which evolved into the religion of Buddhism – are pretty much standard fare in the long history of man's quest for salvation. The Buddha recognised 'Four Noble Truths'. The first is simply that life is unsatisfying. The second is that life is unsatisfying because we keep trying (and failing) to satisfy our desires. The third is that there is a way to escape all this dissatisfaction, to achieve salvation. The fourth is a list of rules we should follow. Known as the 'Eightfold Path', this list includes various prescriptions on how to live well, and, most importantly, how to achieve salvation through meditation.

Some forms of Buddhist meditation involve focusing intensely on the illusoriness of the self and the world. This illusoriness is, supposedly, the source of our dissatisfaction. We are dissatisfied partly because we try to 'attach' our non-existent selves to objects and situations, and partly because we fail to see that the impermanent world of maya is a veil of deception. When we have successfully achieved a sense of selflessness and worldlessness, we enter a blissful state known as 'enlightenment' or 'nirvana'. Salvation, so it goes, is achieved through acquiring intuitive knowledge of one's complete absorption into the higher power of nirvana.

In outline, nirvana is similar to the idea of Brahman. The reason for the similarity is that, historically, Buddhism emerged out of Hinduism. Most Buddhists agree with Hindus that when we reach salvation we are liberated from an endless cycle of reincarnations. Some Buddhists construe nirvana as a state in which we become aware that everything derives from the same source, a cosmic oneness, like Brahman. And some Buddhists construe nirvana, like Brahman, as an ultimate reality or creative principle.

However, few Buddhists construe nirvana as a universal consciousness. This difference between Brahman and nirvana is hugely significant. Like Kant with his noumenal '$x$', Buddhists are reluctant to attribute too much content to nirvana. But Buddhists say they are reluctant not because they lack knowledge of nirvana, but because they don't think there is anything much there to know. The word nirvana, in its original Sanskrit, means simply 'blown out' or 'extinguished'. In this sense, Buddhism has as much in common with Schopenhauer's philosophy as with Hinduism (Schopenhauer was inspired by both Buddhism and Hinduism). Many Buddhists believe that when we have reached enlightenment, when we have reached a state of selflessness and worldlessness, when we have stopped trying to attach ourselves to reality, when we are no longer experiencing dissatisfaction, we will have reached a state of complete 'emptiness'.

According to these Buddhists, there is nothing more to nirvana than a person's realisation that neither the self nor the world exists. Nirvana has no positive content at all; it is pure negativity. In emptiness, nothing is real; there is no self and no world, just a void. This is an example of what I described in chapter two as a none-sided theory of human existence. In the eighth century, the Buddhist monk Te-Shan extolled the virtues of emptiness: 'Only when you have nothing in your mind and no mind in things are you vacant and spiritual, empty and marvellous.'

At face value, the idea that emptiness is the higher power behind our universe seems far from marvellous. By engulfing human existence in negativity, emptiness would overwhelm us in the most dismal way. And in the most implausible way. We could hardly be 'saved' by an empty higher power in which we never existed all along. Nirvana would mean having 'just life enough to enjoy being dead', as the economist Frank H. Knight wittily described it.

Alternatively, perhaps there is more to emptiness than meets the eye. Perhaps emptiness somehow contains the self and the world, despite being neither. Of course, this idea is hard to reconcile with the Buddhist idea that the self and the world are illusory. But many Buddhists have attempted such a reconciliation, no doubt because they are concerned about being overwhelmed by emptiness. Indeed, the very existence of an alternative word for nirvana, namely, enlightenment, indicates a desire among Buddhists to retain the human self and its world; *who* exactly is enlightened, if not a living human being? The Buddha himself insisted there are 'two truths': the 'conventional' truth of human existence, and the 'absolute' truth that everything is empty. Similarly, the Buddhist text known as the *Heart Sutra* explains that 'emptiness does not differ from form' – in other words, emptiness *is* a self and a world, as well as being empty.

The problem is, we already know that the self and the world are neither the self nor the world. If emptiness is defined as neither the self nor the world, and both, then it adds nothing to human existence. Emptiness would be underwhelming as a higher power. Enlightenment would become a description of a situation we're already in.

Now *there's* an idea.

## Existential Homecoming

Dolly Parton once entered a Dolly Parton cross-dressing lookalike competition ... and lost. Even her fellow contestants failed to notice that their heroine was in their midst. 'All these beautiful drag queens had worked for weeks and months getting their clothes,' Parton recalled, 'so I just got in the line and I just walked across ... but I got the least applause.' People seem to find it hard to recognise inspiration even when it's right under their noses.

Can it be true, as some Buddhists say, that human beings are already in enlightenment? Does human existence already contain all the inspiration anyone could ever need? Do we need a higher power at all? When existential refugees seek salvation, are they seeking something that was available to them all along, right here, right now?

If by 'salvation' we mean reaching a place beyond the self and the world, then the answer is no – salvation must always elude us, because a higher power must always be overwhelming or underwhelming. We cannot be saved by a higher power if we don't exist outside of that higher power, or if that higher power doesn't exist beyond human existence.

But this last option points towards an intriguing possibility: perhaps, without going anywhere, we can achieve something almost as good as – or perhaps even better than – salvation. Perhaps there is such a thing as *nowvation*, as it were. Perhaps human beings are already in enlightenment, because nowvation is staring us in the face.

After all, if the self and the world cancel each other out – if both means neither – then we're already in the kind of place sought by existential refugees. Embracing the self and the world means embracing neither, and embracing neither means embracing the self and the world. Nowvation is salvation without the salvation. Practically speaking, we can choose to marginalise the self or the world any time we like, without going anywhere. By giving prominence to one or the other, we can make one or the other recede. In self-awareness, we can make reality recede behind the prominence of the self; in flow, we can make the self recede behind the prominence of reality.

When we assess human existence on its own terms, rather than looking longingly over its shoulder, we can appreciate that being here now is, well ... marvellous! A higher power that was indistinguishable from human existence would be underwhelming, but that doesn't mean that human existence is itself underwhelming. Look around at this vast universe of ours, with its billions of galaxies, each containing billions of incandescent stars. Even the minuscule speck of dust upon which we live, planet Earth, contains more splendour than any of us can ever witness in a lifetime: soaring mountains, roaring oceans, teeming forests, sweeping plains – all bursting with life and colour and sound and beauty. What more could we ask for?

Never mind our futile quest to understand a higher power; the here and now already contains plenty for us to get our heads around. The mysteries of existence are so much more inspiring when approached through nowvation than through salvation. Unlike mystics, we don't need to shut off our worldly senses when we are contemplating the unknown or turning the unknown into knowledge. And unlike captor-bonded believers cowering before God, we don't have to shy away from asking penetrating questions. Albert Einstein, perhaps the greatest scientist ever, insisted that the knowable universe is a more than adequate substitute for a human-like higher power: 'I don't try to imagine a personal God,' he said, 'it suffices to stand in awe at the structure of the world.'

There are also many marvellous things that we ourselves can create in the here and now. Science, poetry, literature, music, comedy, art, architecture, sporting excellence, justice, technology and, yes, love – these worldly achievements are far more edifying than the spectacle of the world's existential refugees scrambling blindly for a non-existent exit door while bickering endlessly amongst themselves about whose imaginary higher power is worthiest.

Of course, life is often unsatisfying. Pain, sadness, loss, disappointment, injustice – in a word, suffering – blows through life like a bitter wind. But, when you think about it, suffering gives us no reason to seek perfection in salvation. Striving for achievable results is always better than hankering after the impossible. The existence of suffering gives us a reason to embrace the here and now, and to wage war against suffering – whether our own suffering or each other's – rather than to quit, as though victory could ever be secured by running away. Nowvation is our only source of hope when the only alternative is the spurious hope of salvation. And when real hope runs dry, as it must from time to time, we can console ourselves with the thought that suffering is the price we pay for the marvellousness of existence.

One day, of course, all of us will pay the ultimate price. All things are impermanent, human beings included; death is unavoidable. But our awareness of death ought to inspire us to appreciate life all the more. If death is bad, then life is good, and existential refugees ought not to flee. Granted, when a loved one dies, there are few consolations to be found in the here and now, other than the consolation of celebrating a life that once was. But perhaps we may also find solace in the idea that, even without a higher power, we will one day reunite with those we have lost. When our self flickers out of existence, we will return to the single reality from which we all came; we will return to the oneness of the universe itself.

Above all, nowvation means freedom – real freedom, not the phoney liberation sought by existential refugees. Losing oneself in a higher power is hardly liberating. Nor is prostrating oneself at the jackbooted feet of an existential captor. Of course, freedom through nowvation isn't unlimited; if salvation is impossible then we cannot escape from this universe, with its relentless imposition upon our plans. But freedom without limits would be meaningless. Freedom is defined by its limits, as surely as up is defined by down. And, in any case, if there's no place to which we can escape from our universe, then our universe is certainly not a prison.

In Buddhism there is a story of a student who asked a Buddhist Master, 'What is the method of liberation?'. The Master replied, 'Who binds you?'. To which the student responded, 'No one binds me'. Suddenly the penny dropped; the student became enlightened. He got there by giving up on trying to escape.

Another Buddhist Master intoned that any monk who has attained enlightenment 'goes to hell as straight as an arrow'. The Master's point, as I see it, is that we cannot *acquire* enlightenment if we already possess such a thing, in the here and now. Ironically, the only impediment to being enlightened is the belief that enlightenment is something we do not already possess.

Such is how I interpret the Buddhist doctrine of emptiness: enlightenment is available to us in the here and now because human existence is already neither a self nor the world; it is already empty. Enlightenment comes from abandoning one's quest for salvation and instead embracing nowvation, the here and now.

Not all Buddhists would agree with me on this. Many Buddhists are ardent existential refugees who believe that enlightenment is something to be striven for, something truly beyond the self and the world – something more like nirvana than nowvation (the word enlightenment being ambiguous between the two, shall we say). These Buddhists take very literally the doctrines of no-self and maya; nowvation, they say, is not only undesirable but impossible. Some of these Buddhists argue that we cannot already be in enlightenment, because enlightenment is a major event in a person's life. Surely you cannot achieve a profound personal transformation if, in doing so, you realise you are no different from anyone else, or from the self you have already been?

I'm not so sure.

Imagine a person who was returning home from his travels, after searching far and wide for a happiness that had eluded him when he was at home; a person who, upon approaching home, suddenly realised that he had felt happier at home than he ever did when he was on the road; that he had taken for granted many of the good things about his home life. Upon arriving home, this person would be elated, excited, wide-eyed; he'd be seeing anew the things that he always saw. We might even say that his realisation that he didn't need to flee his home to find what he was looking for was an *enlightening* experience.

According to this interpretation, Buddhist enlightenment involves a profound transformation because, when an existential refugee returns home, he realises the significance of what he tried to leave behind. And, through this realisation, he becomes different from the ordinary folk who stayed at home. His appreciation of home becomes deeper than theirs; you don't know what you've got till it's gone.

One of my favourite Buddhist verses celebrates the idea that enlightenment is a form of homecoming – *existential homecoming*, shall we say:

> *Misty rain on Mount Lu,*
> *Waves surging on Che-chiang;*
> *When you have not yet been there,*
> *Many a regret surely you have.*
> *But once there and homeward you wend,*
> *How matter-of-fact things look.*
> *Misty rain on Mount Lu,*
> *Waves surging on Che-chiang.*

The idea of existential homecoming can also be seen in an otherwise peculiar practice of some Buddhist monks. When asked to describe nirvana, Buddhist monks (especially in the Zen tradition) sometimes offer curt but portentous descriptions of proximate objects and scenes: 'dumpling', a 'blossoming branch of the plum', the 'cypress-tree in the courtyard'. How can banal observations such as these be profound? The reason is that nowvation is profound. When enlightenment is all around us all the time, a dumpling is more significant than any higher power.

Existential homecoming also explains why Buddhists often adopt a solemn and reverential manner when performing banal tasks. Performing an everyday practical task with great awareness and deliberateness couldn't be further from rejecting the here and now. And the opposite of rejecting the here and now is, some Buddhists would say, the definition of enlightenment. When performed attentively, tasks such as raking leaves, sawing wood, cleaning windows, pumping up tyres, washing the floor, sewing on buttons, making a pot of tea, and so on, become a form of meditation through which enlightenment can be achieved.

Take the opportunity to reflect on the profundity of your everyday experience by performing a mundane practical task mindfully. Whichever task you choose, try to experience this familiar task anew, with a fresh awareness, as though you were coming back home to the marvellousness of being here now. Really *notice* what it feels like to engage practically with the world. Notice the amazingness of … normality.

For instance, you might decide to do the washing up mindfully. You'll feel the warm water flowing gently like ribbons down your fingers, palms and wrists. You'll feel the sponge moving across the surfaces of the pots and pans, sometimes roughly over stuck-on food, sometimes smoothly, as though you were cleaning ice. You'll hear squeaking, trickling, gurgling, clonking, scraping, splashing: what a delicate symphony inside your sink! You've heard this music a thousand times before, yet now, somehow, you'll be hearing it for the first time. You'll see thousands of tiny bubbles clambering over each other, knitting their foamy pattern, until, one by one, they pop, silently.

Not every modern practitioner of mindfulness will agree with me about the profundity of everyday experience. Many people construe mindfulness meditation as a way to escape from the here and now, to connect with a higher power, to see beyond the self and the world into something supposedly better. You will often hear these people complaining that mindfulness has become too 'secular'. Ironically, they seem to have forgotten how miraculous life is. As Zen Master Thích Nhât Hanh wrote: 'Every day we are engaged in a miracle which we don't even recognise: a blue sky, white clouds, green leaves, the black, curious eyes of a child – our own two eyes. All is a miracle.'

We all flee from existence sometimes. Some will argue that this urge of ours is so deep and enduring that there must be something I've overlooked that could salvage the idea of a higher power. Perhaps they're right; but, personally, I no longer believe that the idea of a higher power is worth any effort. The fraught journey of an existential refugee, I believe, can only ever end in nowvation, in calmly embracing life, in mindfully engaging with the here and now, rather than in salvation. Through coming home, we realise how marvellous, amazing, profound and delightful human existence can be.

However, as our senses awaken, as we see our lives afresh, with a renewed sense of wonderment, we suddenly become aware, like never before, of the oldest and most familiar mystery. I'm talking about the ultimate mystery; the mystery of why anything exists at all.

## The Conquest Over Nought

Winston Churchill once described Russia as 'a riddle wrapped in a mystery inside an enigma'. I don't know if he was right about Russia, but Churchill's phrase is an apt way to summarise where we have arrived at in this chapter, and where we still have to go. By now, we have unravelled the enigma which is the so-called higher power that governs our universe. Having done this, we are ready to confront head-on the most vexing mystery in the whole of philosophy: the question of why anything exists at all. Once we have tackled that mystery, there is one last promise I must make good on: I will explain to you the solution to the riddle of the strange hallucination I described at the start of this chapter. All these discoveries, I will show finally, were hiding in plain sight, in mindfulness, all along.

Why does anything exist at all? At first sight, the tsunami-like force of this question isn't obvious. Normally when we ask why a state of affairs exists, we assume that the answer will involve a prior state of affairs whose existence caused the state of affairs in question. For instance, the answer to 'Why does this book exist?' is that I wrote it. And the answer to 'Why do you exist?' is that your parents conceived you.

However, when we ask the question of why anything exists at all, prior causes are elusive. In effect, we are asking why there isn't nothing. We are saying: something exists, but why didn't nothing exist instead? Why indeed! There doesn't seem to be anything inconceivable or incoherent about nothingness; there might have been nothing. So why is there something rather than nothing? The mind flounders amid the startling power of this question. Nothingness can't explain why there is something, because only nothing can come from nothing. And an already existing cause can't explain why there is something, assuming that the existence of this cause itself remains unexplained. Nothing can come from nothing, yet something obviously exists. *So why is there something rather than nothing?* Pondering this question has the potential to 'tear the individual's mind asunder', warned the astronomer Sir Bernard Lovell.

And, of course, it's not just any old something that exists. There's a whole universe of existence. When we ask why anything at all exists, we're asking why there is a universe rather than nothing.

According to the most widely accepted astrophysical theory, the universe began some 14 billion years ago in a huge cosmic explosion. During this so-called 'Big Bang', all of space and time and matter were flung out from an infinitely small and dense dot known as a 'singularity'. There is plenty of scientific evidence that the Big Bang happened, yet the question of why it happened remains stubbornly unanswered. An explosion cannot be caused by nothing. And if the explosion was caused by *something*, then the existence of this cause would itself require an explanation.

The more you ponder why there is a universe rather than nothing, the more inexplicable the existence of the universe seems. Some philosophers have concluded that the universe just *is* inexplicable. Bertrand Russell, for instance, opined: 'I should say that the universe is just there, and that is all.' Similarly, Sartre believed that existence is 'absurd' – without reason or explanation for its being.

In the face of such a mind-sundering task as explaining why the universe exists, it is tempting to invoke the help of a higher power. But, alas, we already know, due to the overwhelming-underwhelming dilemma, that a higher power cannot be the source of the universe. And, in any case, it is debatable whether any higher power could explain its own existence, let alone the existence of anything else. For instance, if the higher power is construed as conscious – say, as mind dust, God or Brahman – we might reasonably ask why this consciousness exists rather than nothing. Similarly, if the higher power is construed as mysterious, we might ask why this mystical realm exists rather than nothing (and we should be sceptical of any mystic who claims that he knows but cannot say why the mystical realm exists: an ineffable explanation isn't much of an explanation). And if the higher power is construed as empty, we might ask whether it even exists at all.

The only higher power with a fighting chance of explaining its own existence is mathematical truth. If mathematical truths are necessary, then these truths cannot not be true. But, even if we accept that mathematical truths are necessary (as opposed to quasi-necessary, or non-necessary), we needn't believe in the existence of an abstract mathematical realm. Some philosophers argue that mathematical truths aren't *something* at all – rather, they're truths that any object would have to live up to *if* it existed. Thankfully, we don't need to tie ourselves in knots worrying about the precise status of mathematical truths: they can't explain the existence of the universe, because, like any higher power, they'd be overwhelming or underwhelming as the source of our existence.

Some believers argue that God necessarily exists. They say that a universe without a necessary cause is impossible; anything that exists must originate in something necessary, namely, in God. This proposal, however, is riddled with problems. Why can't a universe exist without a necessary cause? Are Russell and Sartre necessarily wrong about the universe? And if God cannot not exist, then how can he also be omnipotent? He can't be omnipotent if he can't stop himself from existing. Moreover, how can God necessarily exist if his non-existence is readily conceivable? Even if we concede that $2 + 2 = 4$ is a necessary truth, 'God exists' doesn't seem to have anything like the same indubitability. Or, to put it another way, 'God does not exist' is not at all like saying '$2 + 2 = 5$'.

Worse still, a necessary God would add fuel to the overwhelming-underwhelming dilemma. If the universe originated in a necessary God, then the universe would – implausibly – be overwhelmed by necessity. Some believers argue that even though God necessarily exists, he is capable of making choices, such as choosing to create our universe, in which case our universe wouldn't be necessary after all; God might have chosen to create something else. But then we might well ask: *why* did God choose to create our universe? Not knowing the answer to this question, we still wouldn't know why our universe exists. And, in any case, can we even make any sense of the idea of a necessary God whose essential nature is to make unnecessary choices?

One final suggestion offered by believers in God is that he is *self-caused*. According to this idea, when we try to understand why God exists we shouldn't look for prior causes, as we would when trying to understand, say, why a book or a person exists. Rather, we should conclude that God alone caused himself to exist. God is capable, so it goes, of overcoming nothingness; he exists rather than nothing because he has the power to bring about his own existence. He completes a 'conquest over nought', as the French philosopher Henri Bergson put it.

Now there's another good idea. If nothing can come from nothing, then, logically, whatever exists must be able to bootstrap its way into existence. The problem is, God fails as a higher power, because, as we know, he is either underwhelming or overwhelming. But perhaps there's another self-causer out there. Perhaps, indeed, we don't need to look very far to find it. Perhaps our very own universe is capable of causing itself to exist. Perhaps the universe is able to overcome nothingness. Perhaps the universe can *impose itself upon nothingness*.

Aha!

The solution to the mystery was obvious all along. We already know, from chapter four, that any existing object imposes itself upon other objects, and is imposed upon by those other objects. Sooner or later every object is imposed upon fatally; every object ceases to exist; everything is impermanent. But until any object is fatally imposed upon, it continues to impose itself upon other objects. In doing so, it also imposes itself upon its own non-existence – upon nothingness. All objects, from the beginning to the end of their existence, exist through imposing themselves upon each other and thereby imposing themselves upon nothingness.

The idea that the universe imposes itself upon nothingness fits nicely with the Big Bang theory. Imposition gives the Big Bang an impetus. The forces involved in that primeval cosmic explosion hurled themselves against non-existence precisely insofar as they antagonised each other. And the result – a universe as vast and powerful as ours – is arguably precisely what we would expect if the universe were something that could impose itself upon nothingness.

To say that a self-causing universe imposes itself upon nothingness is not the same as saying that the universe is absurd. Far from making the universe inexplicable, imposition *explains* why the universe exists. From the evidence of imposition all around us, we can conclude that the universe exists because of imposition. By drawing this conclusion, we give up on trying to explain why nothingness created something. That explanation can never be given, just as 0 can never be made into 1. The universe will always seem absurd if we insist on trying to show how to get something out of nothing, to build a bridge from nowhere. Instead, by looking to existence itself for an explanation for existence, we can build a bridge *to* nowhere; we can connect something with nothing by bringing something to nothing. The end result is the same: a bridge to nowhere is also a bridge from nowhere.

When I think back now to the riddling hallucination I experienced when I was ten years old, I think I understand what it signified. It wasn't about salvation. On the contrary, it was about the *impossibility* of salvation; the blue dot never made it to safety because it never could have done. Above all, my hallucination was about what is left behind when salvation is impossible. Without salvation, without a higher power, imposition is the last word on existence, its essence as well as its explanation. Imposition takes on the trappings of a higher power – the power of conquest over nothingness, and the power to create us and motivate us.

There's one final twist to the story, I now believe. In the symbolism of my hallucination, *the blue dot wasn't me* – not yet, anyway. For the time being, I was the red dot, imposing myself upon nothingness by imposing myself upon the world, as everything that exists must. One day, I'd be fatally imposed upon, as everything that exists must, but until then I ought to embrace being here now, embrace the powers of imposition that govern all of existence. In my hallucination, as in life, my fear blinded me to the truth, filling my head with life-denying ideas of salvation and higher powers. Nowvation was waiting patiently beneath my fear.

By calmly accepting our existence, by mindfully coming home to reality, we can appreciate that the Small Answer to the Big Question 'Is there a higher power?' was hiding in plain sight all along: no. The answer is the last link in a chain of insights. In mindfulness, we calmly behold the self and the world. In doing so, we realise that neither is both and both is neither – emptiness is form. In turn, we realise that a higher power cannot be neither the self nor the world without being overwhelming or underwhelming. In either case, a higher power is unable to provide us with salvation, and therefore is no sort of higher power at all. Existence is imposition through and through; we rise, we fall, and that's all. So much insight from mindfully paying attention to the here and now! As the Buddha concluded, intending, I think, to be taken both literally and metaphorically: 'Life is but a breath.'

By mindfully embracing life, we come to understand how, as human beings, we can harness a unique form of impositional power – the power to choose, the power to impose our freedom upon the world. Schopenhauer was right that there is a Real Rumble, a theatre of conflict in which all things are impermanent, but he was wrong that a blind will is the mystical essence of everything, and he was wrong that we should extinguish our willpower to extinguish everything. Human freedom is unique, and should be cherished and flaunted. Rather than seeking an impossible refuge from life, we should stand up and be counted, fighting against suffering, and fighting to make life even more marvellous.

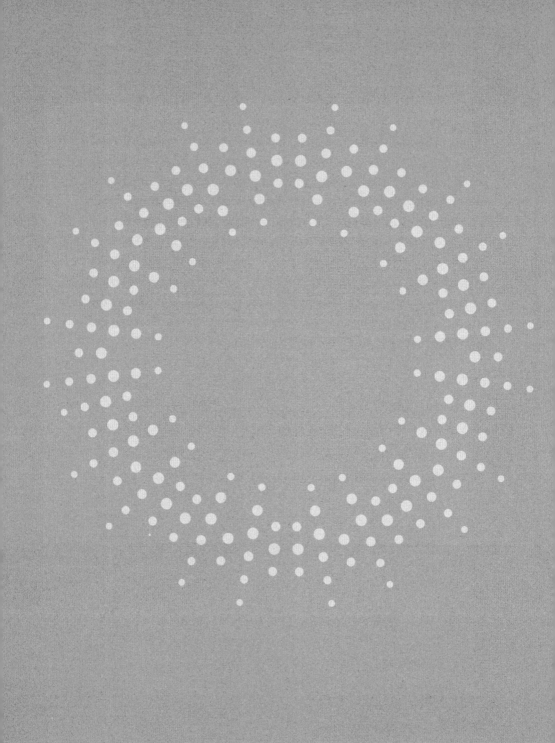

# Six

## What Makes a Life Good?

'Get busy living, or get busy dying.' So said the character Andy Dufresne in the film *The Shawshank Redemption*. Dufresne's advice strikes a chord deep within us, stirring us into an awareness that on this mortal coil of ours we either take steps to improve our lives or we give up and wait to die. But this fundamental choice isn't always as simple as it looks. We're not always sure how to live, how to make things better – there are so many competing views on what a good life is. Amid this welter of words, we do well to remind ourselves of the importance of deeds. And we do well to focus on some simple, homely truths about goodness, truths that belie the idea that we need to hide from our existence to find solace. Mindfulness brings these truths to life.

D o you think you have lived a good life so far? It's an arresting question, one that urges us to pause. So pause, and consider your answer.

Chances are, you had two kinds of thoughts: thoughts about whether you've been happy, and thoughts about whether you've been morally good. In the first category, you might have recalled some happy scenes in your life – a fresh snowfall, a birthday party, a moment of intimacy. In the second category, you might have recalled some times when you performed a good deed – helping someone in need, nurturing a child, counselling a friend. You might also have noticed that some thoughts belong to both categories.

These two categories tell us what we mean by a good life: a life full of happiness and morality. But they cannot tell us *how* to live happily or morally. To find this out, we need to know which situations and actions are likely to bring goodness to our lives. This question has been debated for millennia, especially by philosophers and theologians. Uncontentious answers have proved elusive because too many thinkers have tried to discover goodness without facing up to the demonstrable facts of human existence. A better approach would be to seek goodness whilst resolutely reminding ourselves: *I am here now*.

Through this approach, we can learn to steer clear of life-denying philosophical or religious proclamations on the good life, while availing ourselves of some time-honoured common sense on the topic. Much of this common sense has been corroborated by scientists and economists, who in recent years have taken a great interest in the question of what makes a life good. Above all, we can discover goodness through direct experience. We can become happier and more moral by learning to pay mindful attention in the here and now.

## The Pursuit is Happiness

Happiness is a powerful antidote to existential anxiety: a happy person wants to savour his existence, not hide from it. So, to overcome existential anxiety, we just need to aim to be happy, right? Alas, it's not that simple. Existential anxiety encourages us to seek happiness without facing up to being a self in a world. When we aim for this spurious, life-denying kind of happiness, we only succeed in perpetuating our unhappiness.

Some philosophers argue that happiness consists solely in bodily pleasures, whether these pleasures are sensual, sexual, aesthetic or gustatory. This theory is called 'hedonism', in keeping with the colloquial sense of that term. For a hedonist, pleasure is paramount. He pursues what might be called a one-sided, materialist happiness – his self, his consciousness and his freedom are subordinate to his quest for pleasurable feelings, and to the feelings themselves. He behaves like an automaton, programmed only for seeking and experiencing physical gratification.

Some extreme hedonists could even be said to be pursuing a none-sided happiness. They subordinate their self-awareness and their awareness of reality to their quest for pleasure. A particularly lamentable example of this skewed focus can be seen in drug addiction.

As we saw in chapter one, drugs are not the only form of none-sided pleasure. Drinking, gaming, celebrity gossip, social media, television and gambling are all ways in which people experience pleasure without self-awareness or awareness of reality. Some might argue that these other forms of none-sided pleasure can be life-enhancing in moderation. But seeking pleasure without *ever* facing up to one's existence is a futile business. When we kid ourselves that living a pleasurable life doesn't require any conscious effort or realism on our part, we soon find that our pleasures are swamped by an increase in disorder, pain, misery and indeed boredom.

In response to hedonism, many philosophers insist that happiness requires a contribution from the self. There are various philosophical theories that emphasise this point, in subtly different ways. For instance, philosophers who are 'eudaemonists' define happiness as a state in which we routinely reflect on our lives and strive to live in a deliberate and purposeful way. Similarly, philosophers who are 'existentialists' encourage us to recognise that our choices and attitudes influence whether we become happy or not. And philosophers who are 'stoics' argue that we can only be truly happy when we have mastered our feelings and emotions.

Eudaemonists, existentialists and stoics all agree that happiness requires self-control. However, the role of self-control in happiness can be overstated, leading to another implausible one-sided theory of happiness. Philosophers who are 'ascetics' argue that to become happy we should use our self-control to entirely avoid experiencing pleasure, because pleasure, they say, is a threat to our self-control. Obviously, asceticism is not conducive to happiness: a life without any pleasure at all would not be a happy one. And, in any case, most people are incapable of sustaining an ascetic lifestyle. A person who eschews pleasure entirely is likely to lose interest in his mission. He is likely, that is, to 'fall off the wagon', indulging in a spectacular binge of pleasure-seeking, untempered by any self-control at all.

Anyone who has ever, say, studied for an exam, trained for a sporting event or rehearsed for a concert will tell you that the best way to keep up a regime of self-control is to allow oneself occasional, modest pleasures. Pleasure in moderation is a reward for self-control; the reward motivates the effort that justifies the reward that motivates the effort, and so on.

When a self-controlled person allows himself to experience pleasure in moderation, he *loosens* control of himself without losing control. There are echoes here of the concept of remindfulness. A remindful person, you will recall, is someone who enters into a state of flow but, in doing so, equips himself with a reminder to return to mindfulness.

A happy life, in sum, requires a balance of self-control and pleasure. Since we cannot become happy through pleasure without self-control, and vice versa, happiness is best defined as something in between these two mental states: as a mood. Moods are emotions that endure; in turn, emotions tend to be more enduring than pleasures. We cultivate a mood of happiness when we use our self-control to ration our pleasure, and use our pleasure to oil the wheels of our self-control.

Self-control can also make us happy by helping us undermine negative emotions. This is one of the key insights of cognitive behavioural therapy (CBT), as we saw in chapter one. Advocates of CBT point out that our emotions stem from our beliefs: 'the soul becomes dyed with the colour of its thoughts', as the Roman emperor Marcus Aurelius put it. A depressed person, say, might regularly tell himself that he is a failure. By using positive beliefs to refute this negative – surely exaggerated – belief, he may be able to root out his depression, and replace it with a mood of happiness.

Even if we're not depressed, we can cultivate happiness through influencing our beliefs. A powerful and simple way to do this is to count our blessings. Most of us tend not to remind ourselves of the things that are already good about our life, perhaps because we don't want to acquiesce in the status quo. But gratitude doesn't have to mean acquiescence. Gratitude is a basis upon which hope and aspiration can be built. The most fundamental form of gratitude, of course, is to recognise what a privilege it is to exist consciously in this beautiful world of ours.

By deliberately replacing our negative thoughts with positive thoughts, we can make ourselves happier by gradually turning positive thinking into a habit. We can also use external reminders to support our self-control. We can leave little notes-to-self lying around, keep a journal of wise ideas and thoughts, learn to associate inspirational phrases with specific times or situations, or identify heroes whose attitudes we wish to emulate.

None of this implies that happiness requires naive optimism. On the contrary, we have to be realistic to be happy. Psychologists have found that when we understand the reality of a situation, our negative emotional responses to that situation are dampened. Moreover, realism encourages us to test our happiness in real-life situations, to ensure that our positive thinking is robust enough to survive life's challenges. Fragile happiness, after all, is not much happiness. Robust positive thinking is known as resilience. If we succeed in being resilient in the face of life's challenges, we may even be able to see these challenges as opportunities rather than threats.

Realism is also important to our happiness because if we do not understand and engage with the world around us, we leave ourselves vulnerable to disorder; there's no point controlling ourselves if we are going to let reality walk all over us. Yet, at the same time, realism can also mean being realistic about our limitations. If we are unrealistic about what we can achieve, we set ourselves up for disappointment. A happy person tries to control what he can control, and doesn't try to control what he can't control: this wise counsel has been rediscovered in countless eras and cultures.

In testing ourselves against reality, we use our self-control to influence not just our thoughts but our actions. We deliberately behave in a way that is conducive to happiness, and, in doing so, we gradually make a habit of being happy. If that sounds trite, it's probably because you already know, deep down, how to be happy. You'll have learned it – or at least *heard* it – from your parents or teachers or trusted friends. The only surprising thing about the best advice on how to be happy is how often we ignore it. Staying healthy, taking regular exercise, having a good night's sleep, eating nutritious meals, holding down a job, working hard, keeping our finances under control, acquiring new skills and knowledge, keeping busy with interesting projects or hobbies, and cultivating mutually supportive relationships with our spouses, partners, families, friends and communities: show me someone who is doing all these things, and I'll show you someone who is happy.

Hobbies and projects are particularly important to happiness, because they provide us with a focal point. They give us something to live for and to look forward to, filling us with positivity. We simply don't have time for negative thoughts when we're busy concentrating on a project – solving little problems, setting out goals or making plans. And occasionally our projects give us a marvellous sense of accomplishment.

Paid work is also hugely important to happiness, even if we don't always love our jobs as we love our hobbies. Unemployed people often feel miserable because they feel they have nothing to get up for each morning, no sense of purpose.

Another pitfall of unemployment is social isolation. Loneliness causes terrible unhappiness. Ironically, when we're lonely we enter into a vicious cycle in which we feel too unhappy to talk to people. Lacking support, we fail to make changes that would make us happier, and we also miss out on the happiness that comes directly from feeling supported. In supportive relationships, we experience a sense of belonging, security, trust and confidence. We also feel valued, which adds to our happiness. Of course, support is not the same as pandering. Criticism can be a form of support. People who are happy together are confident enough in their mutual support that they can offer each other constructive criticism.

Supportive relationships are built on realism. A realistic attitude encourages us to seek the support of people around us and offer them our support. Being supportive can mean conversing with people in a sincere and rigorous way – that is, genuinely engaging with their thoughts and concerns – or it can mean offering practical assistance. In supportive relationships, we get involved in each other's projects; these may even become shared projects, through which we develop a shared happiness.

Alas, in the modern world there aren't as many mutually supportive spouses, partners, families, friendships and communities as there once were; we are witnessing an epidemic of loneliness. We are lonely partly because of mutual indifference. Too many of us spend too much time ignoring the people around us because – you guessed it – we are too busy fiddling with smartphones, gawping at celebrity gossip, playing video games, interacting via social media (or via alcohol), watching television or gambling. None-sided pleasures can kill supportive relationships.

Even when we do relate to each other these days, we don't always do so in a spirit of cooperation. There is far too much one-upmanship around, whereby we try to outdo each other through acquiring and flaunting status symbols, such as flashy cars, trendy designer clothes, lavish home furnishings and expensive jewellery. This culture of one-upmanship probably has a lot to do with the amount of onscreen advertising we are exposed to. Many adverts promise us that we'll look impressive – and therefore, supposedly, feel happier – if we buy this or that product. But it doesn't usually work out that way. Our fixation on status symbols is a futile arms race in which we spend time and money adorning ourselves with pretty much the same status symbols as everybody else, meaning that no one ends up impressed. Meanwhile, we all end up lonelier and unhappier than we would have been if we'd been more supportive of each other.

Of course, not all forms of status-seeking destroy happiness. We can also seek status through earning people's respect, whether through charity, kindness, leadership, art, music, sporting excellence, scientific and technical skill or making people laugh. When we acquire status in these pro-social ways, our happiness is tied to that of others. And through making a contribution to the happiness of others we gain self-respect – as opposed to the self-esteem we get from one-upmanship. People with a lot of self-esteem tend to be agitated, paranoid and combative. People with a lot of self-respect tend to be happy.

An emphasis on the communal aspect of happiness can be taken too far, however. Happiness researchers have found that a key component of a happy society is personal freedom. Under repressive regimes, in which a government forces its vision of happiness upon the population, people are miserable. To be happy, citizens must be free to pursue their own happiness, in their own way, through their own choices and projects, including their choices of which people to associate with and how. And, to some degree at least, people must use their self-control to take responsibility for becoming happy. When people are given the wherewithal and encouragement to pursue their own happiness, they end up more sociable than when a spurious togetherness is imposed upon them by the government. Contemporary politicians – who are spending large sums of public money on trying to measure and increase the national happiness – should take note.

**"Through making a contribution to the happiness of others we gain self-respect"**

Thus endeth the sermon … perhaps to your relief. But you might also be wondering about a peculiar irony of all this. The comments I have made about happiness, togetherness, self-control and responsibility do indeed sound like the sort of thing you might hear at a religious service. Religion often leads people towards a happy lifestyle. There is even some evidence that religious people today are happier, on average, than non-religious people. Religion can give people a purpose, a project (seeking salvation, or partaking in charitable works), a network of social support (through attendance at religious gatherings) and plenty of sensible advice.

There is no denying these facts about religion. But there is also no denying that the motivation for religion is usually existential anxiety. When religious people insist that their quest for salvation makes them happy, they are simultaneously confessing that their existence makes them unhappy; they are existential refugees. Deep down, all existential refugees are motivated by the deepest unhappiness possible. Like captives who fall in love with their captor, religious people convert their unhappiness into happiness only at the cost of deceiving themselves about how they really feel towards life. This is the most fragile happiness possible. It can shatter into intense feelings of torment and shame. It can warp into a fraught ethos of extreme conformism, in which religious captives enforce each other's subservience. And it can open the door to the trauma of abruptly losing one's religion.

Pursuing happiness while facing up to existence is much more effective. Instead of building happiness on the shaky foundation of existential anxiety, we can make happiness the foundation of our lives. Of course, that's not to say that we should deny others the opportunity to practise religion; only that we can embrace – and offer – a positive alternative.

## Moral Distraction

The fact that we can become happy through cultivating mutually supportive relationships hints that our parents, teachers and trusted friends were right about something else: we can become happy through being a moral person; it's good to be good. It's obvious why, when you think about it. Typically, being good encourages others to be good to you, which makes you happy. And performing a good deed itself makes you feel happy. The connection between happiness and morality simplifies the task of living a good life. The two kinds of goodness overlap. To some extent at least, we can become happy by being moral, and vice versa.

But to what extent? Is there any more to morality than happiness? Is morality always about supportive relationships? Is it possible for us to support each other's immorality? I would say not: helping each other be immoral would not truly be supportive. So what exactly is morality?

Philosophers and theologians have been debating this question for millennia. The only thing they seem to agree on is that it's good to debate the meaning of morality. There are three main kinds of theory in contention: those that define morality in a life-denying way; those that deny morality exists at all; and those that define morality in a life-affirming way. Let's explore some of these various theories.

According to life-denying theories of morality, to find moral goodness we need to look beyond human existence – that is, beyond the self and/ or the world. In this way, seeking moral goodness becomes a distraction from existence – *moral distraction*, it could be called.

Alternatively, theories that deny the existence of morality encourage us to pay no heed to so-called morality. In so doing, they, too, distract us from our existence, or, at least, from aspects of our existence that are relevant to morality. These theories offer us *amoral distraction*.

An example of a one-sided form of moral distraction is 'moral perspectivism'. Philosophers who are moral perspectivists argue that morality is a matter for each of us to decide on our own. Morality, so it goes, is in the eye of the beholder; to discover how we ought to behave, we needn't look beyond our own minds. Obviously, this theory is ludicrous; plenty of evil people have thought they were morally good. Morality cannot be equated with an individual's opinions and choices.

Some philosophers accept this, while still insisting that morality is in the eye of the beholder. In other words, these philosophers say, morality is a fiction, a figment of our imaginations. When we make moral pronouncements, so it goes, we are using them as a fig leaf for our naked self-interest. This form of amoral distraction could be called *amoral perspectivism*. It encourages us to consider only ourselves when we decide how to behave. A quick test of the sincerity of amoral perspectivists would be to threaten to lock them up on the basis that they're a threat to civilisation. They'd soon tell us we were definitely in the wrong.

The opposite form of one-sided moral distraction could be called *moral determinism*. According to a moral determinist, individuals have no conscious control over whether they behave morally; our conduct arises solely from how our brains and bodies interact with the circumstances we find ourselves in. We can learn moral behaviour, the moral determinist insists – we can, perhaps, learn to replace some of our baser instincts with civilised conduct – but we have no control over this learning process; learning is itself entirely a product of our circumstances. Obviously, moral determinism is ludicrous too. It equates people with animals – always passive respondents, never active and free agents capable of freely chosen, self-guided learning. No animal – not even a trained one – is capable of genuinely moral behaviour.

Indeed, implicitly accepting this, some determinists deny that morality exists at all. All that exists, they say, are the various material or social forces that determine our behaviour. This form of amoral distraction could be called *amoral determinism*; like moral determinism, it distracts us from the fact that we can freely choose to behave morally. We could test the sincerity of amoral determinists by threatening to lock them up and subject them to a regime of corrective training. Before the training even started, they'd tell us we were in the wrong.

Another example of moral distraction is 'collectivism'. A collectivist insists that moral goodness always consists in what *we* should do. By delegating every obligation to everyone in his group, the collectivist distracts himself from his own freedom, and from reality. The group knows best, he tells himself. In doing so, he also distracts others from his own moral distractedness. By invoking collective obligations, he *seems* to care about morality, even as he hides from life; indeed, he seems to take morality more seriously than any individual in his group ever could. The bigger and more powerful the group he delegates to, the more convincing his moral pronouncements sound. Hence, the collectivist often fixates on the morality (or otherwise) of governments: governments represent the whole of society and wield huge power. The collectivist bathes in the reflected glory of the kind of moral government 'we' as a society could supposedly create.

Some philosophers advocate an extreme form of collectivism known as 'postmodernism'. According to the postmodernist, the whole of society contains not only all of morality but all of *everything*. There is no reality beyond society, so it goes, and there are no individuals beyond society; our society mistakenly believes that the self and freedom exist, and mistakenly believes that there is a real world beyond our shared beliefs. To create a morally better world, the postmodernist says, we need to change society; we need to stop believing that we exist as individuals and stop believing that our shared aspirations are constrained by reality.

Postmodernism is a bizarre blend of moral determinism, moral perspectivism and idealism. According to the postmodernist, our morality is always the morality of our society (moral determinism) but we collectively choose this morality (moral perspectivism) just as we create our 'reality' through our shared beliefs (idealism). We all belong, so it goes, to a nebulous moral ether that contains no reality and no individuals. For all its eclecticism, postmodernism amounts to a none-sided theory of existence, and a none-sided kind of morality. Society and morality are nothing without individual people and a real world.

Incredibly, postmodernists consider themselves to be at the vanguard of human progress. But, in fact, their worldview is a throwback to totalitarianism, the deeply regressive political ideology that wreaked havoc in the middle of the twentieth century when postmodernism first emerged. Totalitarian regimes, including those of communists and fascists, use government force to subsume the individual into a spurious collective morality. And invariably these regimes show a callous indifference to reality, especially the reality of their policies' disastrous effects, including the economic decline and misery that intrusive governance causes. When the moral betterment of society depends on believing in the non-existence of individuals, individual lives don't matter; anyone who opposes the consensus becomes both immoral and dispensable. Totalitarians have murdered tens of millions of people throughout history.

We should bear in mind this brutal history whenever we hear people today blithely champion collectivism. There is nothing wrong with contributing to the common good – far from it – so long as we remember that society is comprised of conscious individuals. We can improve society only by improving the lives of individuals. And society can only be improved *by* individuals. Morality is nothing unless individuals behave morally.

Collectivism is more widespread than you might realise. It crops up, for instance, in the idea that everyone and everything belongs to a single, conscious higher power – a universal consciousness (whether God, Brahman, nirvana or whatever). People typically adopt a tone of righteousness when championing this idea. They assume that believing in a universal consciousness is a morally good thing to do. Surely, they say, we'd all be nicer to each other if we knew we shared the same consciousness? We'd realise that mistreating each other is equivalent to mistreating ourselves.

I'm not so sure. Believing in a universal consciousness might also encourage us to behave egocentrically. If other people are ultimately the same as us, we might as well treat them as we want to be treated, not as *they* want to be treated. For instance, if I like eggs, and you hate eggs, and I believe you're the same as me, I might as well make you an omelette.

Or, indeed, I might as well not care how *I* ought to behave. Why should I care about my behaviour if I don't really exist and neither does the world, including you? There is a big difference between the (uplifting) idea that we're all fellow human beings and the (dismal) idea that everyone and everything belongs to a homogenous cosmic 'we'. Like any form of collectivism, a universal consciousness provides moral distraction. A person who believes that moral goodness arises through his submersion into a cosmic 'we' is distracted from his existence, and others are distracted into thinking that he is moral.

This verdict may sound harsh, but, in fact, plenty of religious people insist that when we become aware of our cosmic oneness we do not become morally good. Some Buddhists, for instance, insist that there is nothing morally good about enlightenment; on the contrary, they say, to become enlightened we must go *beyond* morality. To connect with the cosmic oneness of nirvana, so it goes, we must *stop* trying to be good. It is doubtful that the Buddha himself would have agreed with this claim. Nonetheless, various Buddhist Masters have advanced it, such as Seng Ts'an:

> *If you want to get the plain truth,*
> *Be not concerned with right and wrong.*
> *The conflict between right and wrong*
> *Is the sickness of the mind.*

Similarly, Chuang Tzu noted that, as far as enlightenment is concerned, 'vain struggles after charity and duty to one's neighbour' are as futile as 'beating a drum in search of a fugitive'.

The idea that we need to go beyond right and wrong to reach an amoral higher power is a frequent theme in mysticism. We can reach a blissful state, some mystics say, only if we escape from life, and we can escape from life only if we stop trying to live in a morally good way. I can hardly think of a more dismal idea than this mystical form of amoral distraction. It's like telling people: 'To achieve bliss, all you have to do is run away from your shadow, and not give a damn about anyone else. Ready, steady, go!' Some mystics, including some Buddhists and Taoists, have the chutzpah to suggest that *after* we have reached an amoral higher power we will automatically become good in the here and now, as a sort of by-product – as though, say, we could lose weight as a by-product of getting fat.

Other mystics do aim to achieve moral goodness, but they maintain that we can achieve it only by going beyond the self and the world. The mystical realm, these mystics say, is the source of all goodness; only by tapping into this source can we become good. Plato, for instance, thought that morality, like mathematical truth, exists in an abstract realm that we can access only through intuition. This mystical kind of moral distraction is only slightly less dismal than the idea of an amoral mystical realm; either way, seeking moral goodness in the here and now is futile.

Of course, it would be wrong to suggest that all religions – Eastern, Western or otherwise – are indifferent to the idea of living a moral life. Most religions provide extensive instructions on how we should live and treat each other. For most religious people – including some Buddhists – we can only connect with a higher power if we are morally good in the here and now. Some religious people argue that morality originates in a higher power – for instance, in God – and reaches us via a series of instructions on how we can return to that higher power by emulating its moral goodness.

However, the fundamental problem with religious moral guidance is the same as the problem with religious advice on how to be happy. Underpinning all such pronouncements is existential anxiety, like an alarm going off, telling religious people to abandon their existence. When religious people encourage each other to be good, their encouragement has a dark side; they are telling each other that good behaviour is good not in itself but because it leads to a higher power. Good behaviour is construed as an escape route.

And not all escape routes are good. For instance, in most religions 'good behaviour' includes a medley of rituals which – though they might be inherently enjoyable – don't actually add any moral goodness to the world. Praying, lighting candles, offering blessings, and so on – these activities amount to moral distraction, an opportunity for a religious person to bathe in the reflected glory of a higher power whose so-called morality exists beyond the here and now.

And some escape routes are downright bad. The religious idea of goodness can open the door to fundamentalism – that is, to the idea that callous behaviour is as good as genuinely good behaviour so long as both lead to the same destination. Fundamentalists are existential refugees whose ardour for salvation has blinded them to their immoral conduct. Like a person fleeing a burning building, they clamber over the living bodies of their fellows.

Moreover, even mainstream religious proclamations can be patently immoral. The various holy books endorse between them all manner of evil actions, from scapegoating and stoning to robbery and rape. Indeed, in the Abrahamic religions, God himself misbehaves prolifically. Perhaps we should expect nothing less of a captor.

No doubt, there will be plenty of moderate religious people who will admit that their favoured religious texts contain many outdated and dubious moral instructions, as well as many sensible ones. Fair enough. But, as Richard Dawkins has observed, if a person can cherry-pick the sensible moral instructions of his religion, he cannot be getting his sense of right and wrong from his religion; he must be getting his morality from elsewhere. He must be getting it from the same place that all moderate religious people get it from, these moderates having alighted on the same sensible morality despite the many differences between their religions. In the end, all these moderates must be getting their morality from the same place as non-religious people: from the here and now.

At its worst, religion displays the same fundamental shortcoming as any life-denying theory of morality and any morality-denying theory of life: the discouragement of *responsibility*. Responsible people face up to their existence; they are aware of their freedom, and of reality. They are aware that doing the right thing means making choices that have moral outcomes in the here and now. They are aware, in other words, that morality is nothing without action – not ritualistic action, or action designed to help us achieve salvation, but action performed for its own sake. They are aware that luxuriating in a collective 'we' does not make us moral; to be good, we must be good *to* individuals *as* individuals.

How could it be otherwise? Morality is life-affirming – we all know that! So let's take a look at some life-affirming theories of morality.

## How to Paint the World Moral

If a child asked you what morality is, chances are you'd cite some real-life examples. Helping a blind man cross the road; keeping a promise; saying 'thank you'; that kind of thing. Life-affirming theories of morality employ the same sort of strategy as this, only more systematically. Rather than trying to list every possible example of morality, these theories simplify the task by trying to give a general definition of morality that identifies what *type* of action is morally good. Let's sample some of these theories.

The most popular among them is called 'utilitarianism'. Utilitarians believe that morally good actions are those that create happiness. On the surface, this definition sounds plausible; utilitarianism captures the idea that a world full of morality would be a world in which, largely, people were happy. Utilitarianism also captures the idea that moral goodness is, largely, a practice through which we benefit each other: there are likely to be many instances in which, as individuals, we can make other people happy at a tolerable cost to our own happiness.

However, peering a little deeper, it becomes clear that utilitarianism cannot be the *definition* of morality. The problem is, creating happiness is not always morally good, and moral goodness does not always create happiness. Imagine, for instance, that you discovered a simple cure for the common cold but you shared the cure only with your friends; your action would have created happiness, but would not be morally good. Or imagine that you scolded a toddler who put his finger into a plug socket; your action would have made him unhappy, but you would still have done a good thing.

Responding to these kinds of objection, utilitarians argue that being morally good means not just creating happiness but *as much happiness as possible* – whether among as many people as possible or in the long run.

But this enhanced definition fails, too. There are actions that create as much happiness as possible but aren't morally good. Imagine, for instance, a surgeon who killed a single, healthy patient so as to harvest organs for several transplant patients. Clearly, this action would be wrong, even though it created as much happiness as possible.

Conversely, there are actions that are morally good but don't create as much happiness as possible. Consider someone visiting his grandmother. The time he spends with her is time he could have spent, say, volunteering at the local soup kitchen, or raising money for refugees. He could create a lot more happiness by performing these other actions, but visiting his grandmother is still a morally good thing to do.

Some people might say he has a duty to visit his grandmother. The idea that morally good actions are based on duties is known as 'deontology'. According to deontologists, doing your duty means following various rules of morality. Most of these purported rules concern how we should treat people. On the negative side are such rules as: don't steal, don't lie, don't cheat, don't kill, don't commit harm. On the positive side are such rules as: be kind, be caring, be honest, be fair, be just, be polite. These rules of interpersonal conduct can be (roughly) summed up in a single rule, often called the Golden Rule: *treat others as you would wish to be treated*. Some people say that the Golden Rule is common to all societies and religions (although here I am assuming that the various moral rules derive their authority from culture or reason, not from a supernatural lawgiver).

As well as seeking to identify rules of interpersonal conduct, many deontologists seek to identify rules about how we should treat the natural world. This is one of deontology's strengths over utilitarianism. Morality is not only about how we treat each other. In our dealings with nature, deontologists say, we should follow rules such as: don't pollute, don't kill or cause suffering to animals, don't destroy natural beauty.

Like utilitarianism, deontology seems plausible, yet it cannot be the definition of morality. The problem, once again, is that moral rules don't always lead to good actions, and good actions don't always involve following moral rules. Imagine if a murderer asked you to tell him the whereabouts of his intended victim; in this situation, following the rule 'don't lie' would be morally wrong. Or imagine the situation faced by the Allied governments before the Second World War. For a long period, the Allies upheld the Golden Rule in their treatment of the Nazis, a policy which has become known as 'appeasement' – a morally wrong policy in the circumstances.

Conversely, there are situations in which people perform good actions without following moral rules. Imagine seeing a child drowning in a lake. Chances are, you'd dive in to assist the child without a second's thought. Your action would be morally good, even though you followed no moral rules; you were acting solely on an emotional urge. Or imagine giving your spouse or partner a present on their birthday because you love them. Explaining to them that you are only doing your duty would not only be morally superfluous but positively immoral.

A more fundamental problem with deontology is that moral rules sometimes conflict with each other. For instance, consider the following question: should we fund the construction of a dam to enable some people to access clean water? The rules 'be fair' and 'be caring' suggest we should. But, then again, the various rules about how we should treat the natural world might suggest we shouldn't build the dam. To decide when to follow one moral rule rather than another requires something other than following moral rules.

Perhaps when we are confronted with moral dilemmas we should use our feelings to decide the right thing to do. But this suggestion, once again, can be taken too far. 'Sentimentalists' claim that morality means acting always in accordance with good-natured feelings such as compassion, sympathy and love (although most sentimentalists aren't averse to a bit of righteous anger). The problem is, even good-natured feelings can lead to morally bad decisions – for instance, the compassionate release of mass murderers from prison, or crimes of passion committed out of love. Nor do good actions always involve good-natured feelings. For instance, in medicine and law we actively encourage practitioners to make moral decisions dispassionately.

One final possibility is that morality means having a virtuous *character*. According to this theory – known as 'virtue ethics' – moral actions are actions that display virtuousness, and virtuousness is something we must learn through instilling good habits in ourselves. There are many different virtues, so it goes, ranging from feelings to intellectual abilities via something in between. Compassion, friendliness, courage, mercifulness, quick-wittedness, modesty, loyalty, temperance, assertiveness, patience, gratitude, tactfulness, truthfulness, preparedness – these are just a few examples.

As you can see, some of the virtues resemble internalised versions of moral rules; other virtues involve emotions, the likes of which sentimentalists would approve of. In the end, though, the problem with virtue ethics is familiar too. Not all virtuous actions are morally good: for instance, loyalty to a dictator; courage that puts others in danger; false modesty; excessive unselfishness (charity, as they say, begins at home). And not all morally good actions are virtuous; otherwise, how could we become virtuous in the first place? To instil virtuous habits in ourselves, we need to be able to perform moral actions despite our initial lack of virtuousness.

None of the life-affirming theories of morality have led us to a comprehensive definition of moral goodness. The best we can do is say that *many* instances of creating happiness, following rules, acting sentimentally or displaying virtue are morally good. We can even say, in specific instances, that an action was morally good *because* it involved creating happiness, following a rule, acting sentimentally or displaying virtue. In turn, some people might go as far as to say that all moral actions involve one of those four types of action. But what we cannot do is identify a specific type of action that is always morally good. Moral goodness resists definition.

This sounds like a negative conclusion. But a dead end can also be a beginning, a change of direction. In 1903, G.E. Moore proposed a brilliant new theory of morality. Moore, as you recall, was the philosopher who rejected scepticism by holding out his hands and saying, in effect, 'reality exists: you can *see* it'. His approach to morality was similarly commonsensical. Moral goodness, he said, is something we can see, like the colour yellow. And, like the colour yellow, morality cannot be defined.

What Moore was getting at, I think, is that we cannot cite a particular kind of object and say: this is what it means to be yellow. Even lemons and rubber ducks and bananas are, after all, sometimes not yellow. Whenever we are discussing an object, it is never superfluous to ask whether that object is yellow or not. Therefore yellow has no definition; yellow is yellow, that's all. The same goes for morality. We cannot cite a particular kind of action and say: this is what it means to be morally good. Whenever we are discussing an action, it is never superfluous to ask whether that action is morally good or not. Therefore moral goodness has no definition; moral goodness is moral goodness, that's all.

Moore's theory is known as 'intuitionism', the idea being that moral goodness is intuitive because it cannot be adequately put into words. This doesn't mean that seeing moral goodness requires us to access a hidden mystical realm. Our moral intuition illuminates the here and now. On this earthly plain (or in our mind's eye), we can plainly see what we ought to do – or, retrospectively, what we ought to have done – and we can see similar obligations in other people. In turn, we can use our moral intuition to identify actual examples of moral goodness – that is, examples of when what ought to have been done was done.

Intuitionism doesn't imply that we're always right about morality. Sometimes our moral intuition misleads us, just as sometimes we mistakenly see yellow. And sometimes moral truth is not obvious to behold. For instance, goodness can be blended with badness, just as yellow can be blended with, say, red. Sometimes we may perceive that an action is only *slightly* good, as opposed to very good, just as we may perceive a shade of yellow that is pale as opposed to strong.

Sometimes, indeed, we may be in such a turbulent situation that we can barely make head or tail of anything, including what we ought to do. To help us see moral goodness, we can use the various other life-affirming theories of morality as rules of thumb. They can point us in the right direction, towards likely examples of moral goodness, just as a person who seeks yellowness might look for lemons, bananas or rubber ducks. We can also use these theories – and, in general, we can use *reason* – to alert each other to potential errors of moral intuition. Sometimes a person with an erroneous moral view might not have seen various aspects of a situation. Helping him to appreciate the fuller picture might help to change his mind.

And, of course, to see more clearly what we ought to do, we can heighten our awareness: we can be mindful.

## Meditate, for Goodness' Sake

Why do meditators have a reputation for being somewhat sanctimonious? Perhaps it's because they keep insisting that meditation has made them better people. Yet, in other contexts, listeners normally feel inspired when they hear tales of happiness and moral improvement. I think the main reason some people are cynical about meditation is that not all meditators are entirely sincere. Not all forms of meditation are genuinely life-improving; some are life-denying. Life-denying meditation encourages people to live in a way that makes them neither happy nor moral.

For instance, as we have seen, when people meditate as a means of achieving salvation – that is, when they meditate on the idea of nirvana, Brahman, God, a mystical realm or any other higher power – they are simultaneously admitting that their existence makes them unhappy. In turn, their meditation reinforces their existential anxiety. They may feel blissful *while* they are meditating, but they meditate because they are unhappy with life. When they emphasise the blissful side of this equation, they protest too much, as it were.

In other instances, the unhappiness caused by life-denying meditation is more overt. Some people, as we have seen, meditate in order to 'lose themselves', or – which amounts to the same thing – to lose their sense of attachment, that is, their urge to impose themselves and their projects upon reality. These meditators recognise, correctly, that trying to change what they can't change is a recipe for unhappiness. But their strategy of never trying to change what they can change is no less disheartening. Drifting through life leaves them at the mercy of a merciless universe. Unhappiness comes effortlessly; happiness doesn't. Being happy requires an effort to improve on reality, and to improve ourselves through consciously shaping our actions and habits.

Some people who meditate to lose themselves become hedonists. They encourage themselves to delegate all their decision-making to their bodies – bodies that naturally seek pleasure as a plant seeks light. In turn, these hedonistic meditators are soon engulfed by unhappiness, by the brambles of chaos, disorder and boredom.

Hedonistic meditators often talk about the importance of 'living for the moment'. To live happily, they say, we shouldn't defer our happiness to a far-off future, and we shouldn't be deterred by the prospect of regretting our actions in future; we should seek to enjoy the here and now, because the present moment is all that ever exists. This ideology was common in the 1960s, when 'spontaneity' was all the rage.

However, the idea of living for the moment is a perversion of the meaning of meditation. It is true that all forms of meditation involve focusing on the present moment. It is also true that meditating teaches us to disentangle ourselves from our thoughts – including our thoughts about the past and the future. But this doesn't mean that, in our day-to-day lives, we should ignore our thoughts about the past and the future. Far from it; these thoughts, like all thoughts, should be *attended* to, and, thereby, deemed either useless or useful. The whole point of disentangling ourselves from our thoughts is that it enables us to replace automatic patterns of thinking with better decision-making – this is the meaning of engaged acceptance.

Good decisions never involve denying reality, including the reality of the past and the future. That's why happiness requires a measure of *deferred gratification* – a recognition that, because the future will one day be the present, we ought not to live only for the present; we ought to plan for happiness. In this way, our happiness becomes a rolling project; we're happy in the present because we planned for our present happiness in the past, and we'll be happy in the future because we're planning for it now.

Not all life-denying forms of meditation encourage hedonism. Some meditators see their practice as a way to support an ascetic lifestyle, with all the unhappiness that entails. The ascetic meditator hides from pleasure, all the better to hide from reality. In this ultimate goal he is not alone. Many meditators believe that meditating is a way to shirk reality. These meditators believe they'll find happiness in the sanctuary of the self. They aim to detach themselves from their thoughts so as to disengage from reality, not engage with it. Their fleeing makes them happy only insofar as reality doesn't.

People who indulge in life-denying meditation tend to meditate too much, by which I mean they live to meditate, rather than meditate to live. In turn, their excessive meditation may exhaust them cognitively, leaving them depleted and more anxious than ever.

And, of course, excessive meditation also uses up time, leaving less time for moral goodness. To be good, after all, means acting in a good way. Sitting alone for hours on end is hardly doing anyone any favours. Life-denying meditators confuse being good at meditating with being a good person. You often hear such meditators argue that meditation is morally good because the problems of the world supposedly stem from everyone rushing around too busily. Sitting still, so it goes, is precisely what the world needs more of. By that logic, we could all make the world a better place by sleeping more, or by locking ourselves in the basement.

The only justification for the claim that meditation makes us morally good would be if meditation has effects which make us morally good. So ask yourself: who would you call upon if you needed help? Would you call upon someone who spent long periods of time in quiet contemplation trying to convince himself that he doesn't really exist, or that the world doesn't really exist, or that neither he nor the world really exists? Would a disembodied, disengaged or distant person be enthusiastically attentive to your worldly needs?

In his excellent book *The Buddha Pill* (co-authored with Catherine Wikholm), Miguel Farias notes the effect that excessive meditation had on his relationships: 'Despite being able to control or even feel unattached from negative feelings – anger, sadness or frustration – I was shocked to find that, sometimes, this lack of attachment made me less sensitive and empathic to other people's feelings ... It was only when a friend joked I was becoming a "meditation junkie" that the penny dropped. He was right; meditation was turning into a way of bypassing real life, or at least of avoiding the parts of it that were difficult or bitter. I had decided then to drastically reduce my practice.'

To the extent that meditation influences a person's day-to-day outlook, a life-denying meditator is, typically, ill-equipped for being good. Granted, there are some life-denying meditators who deliberately practise good behaviour as a complementary means of reaching salvation. You might be able to call upon their moral goodness – so long as they're not too busy seeking salvation by sitting doing nothing.

The confusion of meditation with morality is especially evident among meditators who believe that the practice connects them with a cosmic 'we'. For example, people who practise Transcendental Meditation claim that, through meditating, they are making a positive contribution to the collective consciousness of our species; they are helping, so it goes, to lower our stress levels and increase our interpersonal harmony. The Transcendental Meditation movement has even organised scores of experiments in which thousands of meditators move into an area, meditate for several hours a day, and thereby supposedly improve social relations among the local people, as measured by crime statistics, suicide rates, alcohol consumption and other data. The credibility of these studies can perhaps be indicated by the fact that one such study neglected to mention that there was a fifty per cent increase in homicides during the experimental period. The only thing proven by these studies is how far some meditators will go for moral distraction.

Of course, in highlighting the phoniness of life-denying meditation I am not trying to criticise all forms of meditation. Quite the opposite: I want to immunise life-affirming meditation against the cynicism directed – justifiably – at life-denying meditation. Life-affirming meditation is everything life-denying meditation isn't. Life-affirming meditation is *mindful*, not mindless. When mindfulness meditation is freed from its life-denying roots it becomes unequivocally a force for good.

## Be Mindful, for Goodness' Sake

Some mindfulness exercises explicitly aim to create happiness and moral goodness in the here and now. You can try some of these exercises if you like. For instance, there is a meditation that encourages us to fake a smile or a laugh while focusing on our breathing. The idea is that our artificial positivity will perhaps trigger our brains into releasing happiness chemicals which, in turn, will make us *really* smile or laugh. Worth a try, maybe.

Other mindfulness meditations aim to help us to become more compassionate. For instance, there is a popular meditation in which we are encouraged to think about people we care about, and to mentally project a feeling of compassion towards them. Easy enough, you might think. But there's a canny twist. After we've thought about people we like, we are encouraged to think about people we *don't* like, and to project a feeling of compassion towards them. This is mindfulness as alchemy, turning distrust into kindness.

Another nice exercise in mindful morality involves creating a real con-nection with someone we care about – typically, in this case, a romantic partner. Sitting opposite this person, we are encouraged to meditate while gazing into his or her eyes, and vice versa. This meditation teaches us to be attentive to our partners, to look into their souls.

Alternatively, we can meditate in the company of complete strangers – not necessarily gazing at them, just being together while meditating. This can help us feel comfortable around people, and better disposed to them – including people in general, not just the ones we meditate with.

These goodness-seeking mindfulness exercises are all well and good, but, in a way, they miss the point. To become happier and more moral, we don't need to explicitly try to create these outcomes in meditation. *Any* form of mindful meditation helps us create a mindset that leads us towards a good life. The key is attention. Not the narrow, tunnel vision of the life-denying meditator, with his fixation on hiding from existence, but the expansive, open attention of a meditator who embraces the here and now. Mindful attention has many facets, all of which lead towards goodness.

For instance, as we have seen, in mindfulness we pay attention to ourselves: we become aware of our thoughts, sensations and feelings. In doing so, we create a little clearing in our minds. In that clearing, we can avoid getting tangled up in negative patterns of thinking and behaviour, and we are in a better position to challenge our thoughts, as cognitive behavioural therapy encourages us to do.

In other words, mindfulness leads to self-awareness, which leads to self-control, which leads to better habits of thought and action. In this way, mindfulness helps us to stick to the clean-cut lifestyle that our parents, teachers and trusted friends promised would make us happy. Consider, for example, the relationship between mindfulness and exercise. Mindful people develop the self-control that a regime of regular exercise requires. Some people even combine the two, in yoga or in mindful aerobic exercise.

Mindfulness also means paying attention to *reality*, leading to all the happiness-enhancing benefits of a realistic attitude: staying on top of our lives, keeping busy with interesting projects, avoiding unrealistic ambitions. In mindfulness the attention we pay to reality is both detached and practical; it is practical *because* it is detached. We pay attention to reality so as to *attend* to reality.

Another way in which mindfulness makes us feel happy is by encouraging us to feel grateful for our existence. Our calm self-aware awareness makes us feel glad to be here. In turn, we learn to see none-sided pleasures for what they are: deviations from self-aware awareness. We learn to be wary of these none-sided pleasures. We prefer to consciously savour the here and now rather than unconsciously hide from it. This doesn't mean, of course, that we eschew all pleasures, all the time – only that we ration our pleasures so as to strengthen our self-control, with its overall stewardship of our ongoing mood of happiness. Sometimes, indeed, we may savour our pleasures consciously.

In mindfulness, we live *in* the moment, but not *for* the moment. We don't hide from the future; on the contrary, our expansive attention sees the future, and the past, in the present. In holding our attention steady through time, we attend to the passage of time. In this way, mindfulness helps us plan for the future. Disentangling ourselves from bitter regrets enables us to learn better from the past, and carry this learning forward. And disentangling ourselves from anxious prognostications enables us to make better predictions. We plan for happiness – and we soon arrive there.

As well as leading to happiness, the roads of mindful attention lead to morality. For a start, these roads lead us towards each other – towards a more convivial style of living. In declining to hide from ourselves, or from reality, or both, we are forced to seek solace and assistance in the here and now. And there is no better source of solace and assistance than other people. We *seek* each other's attention when we pay mindful attention.

And we give each other our attention. We attend to each other's needs, worries and interests. We attend to each other's problems in a realistic and rigorous way, whether these problems are psychological or practical. We pay attention, enthusiastically and encouragingly, to each other's projects. We can rely on each other and trust each other: we know we've got each other's backs. Our mindful attention makes us responsible – alert to our surroundings and our obligations.

Mindful attention also makes us empathetic. Recognising the truth of *I am here now* is a basis on which we can recognise that others share our kind of existence – others are here now too, and conscious, like us. Self-aware awareness is like a broadcasting frequency via which we can detect signals from our fellows. By attending to the consciousness of others, we learn to see the world as they see it, and to help them fulfil *their* aims, not ours.

In all of this, mindfulness encourages us to eschew collectivism even while upholding the social solidarity that collectivists profess to value. Descending from the abstraction of a governmental or cosmic 'we', we personally give our attention to real people: real spouses, real family members, real friends, real community members, even real strangers. We help individuals as individuals. Mindfulness often gets flak from collectivists. Perhaps they fear that their moral distraction is threatened by an ethos of real people paying each other real attention. Or perhaps they just don't want to give up on creating a better society on the largest possible scale. Mindfulness reminds us to control what we can control. That way lies not just happiness, but togetherness.

Above all, mindfulness helps us to pay attention to moral truth. The less we hide from our existence, the more we intuitively see what we ought to do, including how we ought to treat this beautiful natural world of ours. And, the more we mingle with our fellows, alertly and attentively, the more we see what we ought to do for them. By following our moral promptings in real relationships, we contribute to a positive cycle in which we catalyse each other's moral behaviour and happiness.

The good life begets the good life — you just need to know where to look for it in the first place. Thankfully, it's right under our noses. The Small Answers to the question of what makes a life good are nothing fancy. Just plain old common sense, the kind of common sense that existential anxiety needlessly turns into a nightmare. Mindfulness helps us see these Small Answers, and to live them — the proof being in the pudding. In this way, *mindfulness* makes a life good.

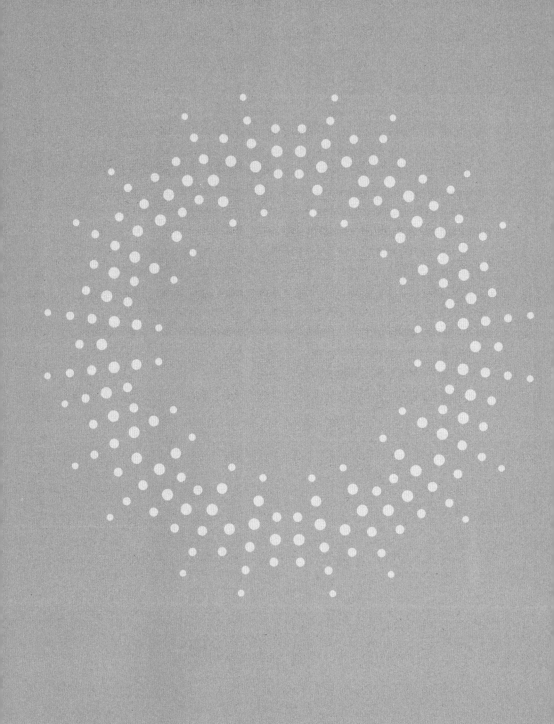

# Seven

...........................................................

# What Does It All Mean?

...........................................................

I cannot tell you what the next chapter contains.
But fear not: you can.

In the cult sci-fi horror film *Cube,* seven people wake up inside a strange, terrifying prison. They have no memory of how they got there. The prison consists of a vast network of room-sized metal cubes. On each side of each cube is a trapdoor, and each trapdoor leads into an adjacent cube. The cubes are empty, although some of them contain hidden sensors that trigger deadly booby traps. As the seven inmates struggle to survive and escape, they are also threatened – in their fear and paranoia – by each other. All the while, they frantically try to grasp the meaning of their predicament. Who put them there? Why them? Why such a grim fate?

I watched *Cube* many years ago, when I was suffering from existential anxiety. Needless to say, the film didn't make me feel any better! I assumed – as presumably most viewers do – that the film was an allegory for human existence. Certainly, existential anxiety feels like being held captive in a terrifying booby-trapped prison. The more you fear your existence, the more you want to escape, the more you ignore your surroundings, the more your interests narrow, the more your horizons shrink, the more you feel boxed in.

*Cube* offers only a few hints as to how the prisoners came to be in their predicament. One of the characters, an autistic mute, manages to exit the prison into a blinding white light. Another of the inmates opines that there was no masterplan behind their capture and imprisonment; everyone involved in the outcome was just doing a job, asking no questions. The prison is a 'forgotten, perpetual public works project', a mere 'accident', he insists, to which his aghast interlocutor responds: 'What have we come to? It's so much worse than I thought.'

It seems to me that these hints represent, respectively, mysticism (the prison has an indescribable explanation) and postmodernism (the prison was created by a social ether that 'we' should radically overhaul). Or perhaps the director, Vincenzo Natali, had something else in mind. My head was teeming with questions and theories about the prison. But there was one thing I didn't question. I didn't question whether the film *is* an apt allegory for human existence.

Imagine standing in one of those cubes, looking around keenly but without thinking about how to escape — just observing. Imagine, under your gaze, the roof sliding off to reveal a twilight sky ablaze with colour. Imagine the cold hard metal floor rippling into a soft meadow, its covering of grass and wildflowers brushing your ankles. Imagine the four walls collapsing outwards, the whole wretched prison structure scattering across the ground in a dice roll of rocks and pebbles. Imagine, now, walking out into the cool, clear air of an alpine plain. A majestic mountain is rising behind you, and, before you, a river is flowing through the valley towards the twinkling lights of a distant city. You follow the river, and soon you come to a marketplace thronging with people. There are voices hollering, bodies bending over stalls, heads nodding, eyes peering, coins clinking as they are passed from hand to hand, awnings flapping, feet scuffling. An artist dabs at her canvas; a busker casts his song into the air; a dog strains at its lead. Meanwhile, in the centre of the marketplace is a fountain, and on its steps people are sitting, standing, chatting, arguing, laughing, gesticulating, smiling, embracing. In their midst is the person you love most in the world, beckoning to you.

No, I don't think *Cube* is an apt allegory for human existence. For most of us, most of the time, life is no prison. Yes, there are booby traps. Each of us will die, in the end. But until then . . .

Until then, what? What is all this *for*? Some people will not be satisfied until they know what their existence means, until they know the reason for their existence, until they know why they awoke in this strange universe with no memory of what came before. For what purpose are we here? Even if our lives were blissful from beginning to end, some people would still want to know: *what is the meaning of life?* Perhaps *Cube* is not such a bad allegory after all.

Have our investigations uncovered any insights that can shed light on the meaning of life? Let's recap.

> "And what it all means boils down to this: the universe exists, and you're in it. That's all"

We have seen that you are here, with your consciousness, freedom and individuality, because your brain has a selfside. As a selfside, you are self-aware, and aware of the world that created you.

We have seen that you are uncertain, because your selfside creates a distance between you and reality, rendering your beliefs as hypotheses and doubts. Yet you can be certain that reality exists – the world relentlessly imposes itself upon you – and you can only be wrong about what you are largely right about.

We have seen that you are free, because your selfside is the opposite of the world's imposition; your freedom is an unworldly force that imposes itself upon reality. You are even free when you are in flow; choosing freedom is a constant option for you.

We have also seen that a higher power cannot exist, unless it overwhelms human existence or adds nothing to it; either way, salvation makes no sense. Thankfully, nowvation is just as satisfying as salvation. And imposition can explain why there is something rather than nothing; ironically, the very force that renders things impermanent explains why things exist.

Finally, we have seen what makes a life good. A good life involves cultivating happiness (through self-control, a realistic attitude, enjoyable projects and supportive relationships) and moral goodness (through opening one's eyes to, and being responsive to, intuitive moral truths).

We have seen all this – quite literally – in mindfulness. The philosophy I have described in this book could be described as *attentionism*. We have validated this philosophy by actually paying mindful attention to our experience. In so doing, we have learned how to overcome existential anxiety. We have learned to challenge the dismal mindset that leads so many people to try to hide from existence – existentially self-absorbed people (who hide from reality), existential self-escapers (who hide from themselves), existential refugees (who hide from both themselves and reality), and people who distract themselves from their existence by indulging in none-sided pleasures.

In turn, through paying mindful attention, we have demonstrated the futility of hiding from life. By calmly facing up to our existence, we have seen that running away from life only makes life seem scarier than it really is. Above all, we have discovered the wisdom I sought right from the start. Attentionism is wisdom. An attentionist is someone who is well informed and well adjusted, someone who looks long and hard at life, who doesn't blink, and who makes the right moves.

And what it all means boils down to this: the universe exists, and you're in it. That's all. So is *that* the meaning of life? Well, no, it can't be. You can't describe the meaning of a situation by simply describing that situation. To do so would be like telling the *Cube* inmates that the meaning of their predicament is ... their predicament; that they're in this place because ... they're in this place. If life is what it is, and nothing more, then there is no meaning of life.

Yet life – being a self in a world – doesn't have to be meaningless. After all, creating meaning is what a self does. When you speak, you *mean* what you say. When you act, you *mean* to act in a certain way. When you create things, you *mean* to change the world. When you encounter other people, you attribute *meaning* to their speech and actions and creations. We are meaning-making creatures. It's in our nature. We can no more avoid making meaning than we can avoid breathing. As we journey through life, we create meaning through the things we say and do – through the relationships and the projects we engage in. All these engagements bring purpose to our existence. They are, indeed, the reason we are here: you get busy living, or you get busy dying.

Could there, in the end, be any other sort of meaning? Shakespeare famously has one of his characters pronounce that 'all the world's a stage, and all the men and women merely players'. But would your life really be meaningful if you were reading from someone else's script? You'd merely be going through the motions; in surrendering yourself to the author's meanings, you'd be rendering your own life meaningless. Even more so if the author was forcing you to read the script – say, if a microchip in your brain was fully determining your behaviour, turning you into a remote-controlled or pre-programmed actor.

Perhaps Shakespeare liked the idea that the world's a stage, because he was the playwright. He brought the most profound and beautiful meanings to his plays and, in doing so, to his life. He wasn't 'merely' a player – and nor should you be. To live meaningfully you have to live deliberately. As the author of your destiny, you too can strive to bring beauty and profundity to your life.

By this I do not mean that you should act as though you live inside a work of fiction. If you never mean to tell the truth, never mean to engage with the real world, never care about your fellows with whom you share that world, then your life will collapse into meaninglessness – it will become 'a tale told by an idiot, full of sound and fury, signifying nothing', to use another of Shakespeare's phrases. Whether you try to lose the world, or lose yourself, or both, seeking meaning beyond the here and now makes your life less meaningful, not more. Existential anxiety drains life of meaning; facing up to existence fills life with meaning.

In the end, asking 'what is the meaning of life?' is misguided and misleading. Meaning is not the sort of thing life itself has. Meaning is what people do, what people make out of life – there are as many meanings of life as there are lives. A better question would be: 'how will I make my life meaningful?' The Small Answer to that question is not so much hidden as *bidden* in plain sight, conjured up by the attention that we pay to our lives. By paying attention to – and by practically attending to – our habits, our projects, our fellows and our surroundings, a meaning of life pours from us like ink from a pen. Mindfulness makes life meaningful.

# Further reading

Chalmers, D., *The Conscious Mind: In Search of a Fundamental Theory*, Oxford, Oxford University Press, 1996.

Cooper, D. E., *The Measure of Things: Humanism, Humility, and Mystery*, Oxford, Oxford University Press, 2002.

Cooper, D. E., *World Philosophies: An Historical Introduction*, Oxford, Blackwell, 1996.

Dalrymple, T., *Life at the Bottom: The Worldview that Makes the Underclass*, Chicago, Ivan R. Dee, 2003.

Dawkins, R., *The God Delusion*, London, Bantam Press, 2006.

Evans, J., *Philosophy for Life and Other Dangerous Situations*, London, Rider, 2012.

Farias, M. and C. Wikholm, *The Buddha Pill: Can Meditation Actually Change You?*, London, Watkins Publishing, 2015.

Heaversedge, J. and E. Halliwell, *The Mindful Manifesto: How Doing Less and Noticing More Can Help us Thrive in a Stressed-out World* , London, Hay House, 2010.

Irvine, B., *Einstein and the Art of Mindful Cycling: Achieving Balance in the Modern World*, Lewes, Leaping Hare Press, 2012.

Layard, R., *Happiness: Lessons from a New Science*, London, Penguin, 2005.

Magee, B., *Confessions of a Philosopher: A Journey Through Western Philosophy*, London, Weidenfeld and Nicolson, 1997.

Musgrave, A., *Common Sense, Science and Scepticism: A Historical Introduction to the Theory of Knowledge*, Cambridge, Cambridge University Press, 1993.

Pinker, Steven, *The Better Angels of Our Nature: The Decline of Violence in History and its Causes*, New York, Penguin, 2011.

Pinker, Susan, *The Village Effect: Why Face-to-Face Contact Matters*, London, Atlantic Books, 2014.

Ridley, M., *The Rational Optimist: How Prosperity Evolves*, London, Fourth Estate, 2010.

Sartre, J-P., *Nausea*, Aylesbury, Penguin, 1965.

Schopenhauer, A., *The World as Will and Idea* (Abridged Edition), London, Everyman, 1995.

Schwartz, J.M. and S. Begley, *The Mind and The Brain: Neuroplasticity and the Power of Mental Force*, New York, HarperCollins, 2003.

Watts, A.W., *The Way of Zen*, Harmondsworth, Penguin, 1962.

# Index

# Acknowledgements

·····················································································

First and foremost, thank you to Rebecca Watts, who commented on my drafts (and my ideas) with the eye and ear of a poet, and gave me tons of good advice and moral support. I couldn't wish for a better ally.

Thanks also to David Cooper, not only for offering helpful comments on my drafts, but for writing some of the books that helped shape how I think about philosophy.

Thank you to Jan and Vic Irvine, for providing both financial assistance and a restorative place to escape to while I worked on this book.

I am also thankful for the financial assistance provided by Hilary and (the late, great) Bill Papworth, and for the hospitality shown latterly by Hilary.

To David Chadwick and his family, thank you for cheering me up when I was worn out.

Finally, thank you to Ivy Press – to Monica Perdoni, for setting up this marvellous opportunity, and to Tom Kitch, for being such a patient, sympathetic and conscientious editor.